P9-CFY-580

Living with Paradox

· ·

H. Newton Malony

. . . .

Foreword by Max De Pree

Living with Paradox

. . . .

Religious Leadership and the Genius of Double Vision

Jossey-Bass Publishers
San Francisco

Substantial discounts on bulk quantities of Jossey-Bass books are available to corporations, professional associations, and other organizations. For details and discount information, contact the special sales department at Jossey-Bass Inc., Publishers (415) 433–1740; Fax (800) 605–2665.

For sales outside the United States, please contact your local Simon & Schuster International Office.

Jossey-Bass Web address: http://www.josseybass.com

 Manufactured in the United States of America on Lyons Falls Turin Book. This paper is acid-free and 100 percent totally chlorine-free.

Library of Congress Cataloging-in-Publication Data
Malony, H. Newton.
    Living with paradox: religious leadership and the genius of double vision/
H. Newton Malony: foreword by Max De Pree.—1st ed.
        p. cm.
    Includes bibliographical references and index.
    ISBN 0-7879-4057-7 (alk. paper)
    1. Christian Leadership. 2. Church management. I. Title.
BV652.1.M35 1998
262'.1—dc21   97-48677
                                                                                    CIP

FIRST EDITION
HB Printing   10 9 8 7 6 5 4 3 2 1

Contents

. . . .

Foreword ix

Preface xiii

The Author xv

1. Religious Leadership and Paradox 1

Part One: Paradoxes in the Religious Leader's Role

2. Person and Position: Being True to Oneself and to
   Congregational Expectations 17

3. Prophet, Priest, and King: Playing Three Roles
   That Become Confounded 31

Part Two: Paradoxes of Perspective

4. Inclusivity and Exclusivity: Appreciating Both
   Uniqueness and Universality in Faith Convictions 45

5. Timely and Timeless: Applying the Bible's Eternal
   Truths to Present Circumstances 59

96391

Part Three: Paradoxes Built into the Structure of Religious Congregations

6. For-Profit and Not-for-Profit: Balancing the Books
    While Serving a Larger Purpose   75

7. Person and Organization: Running an Efficient
    Organization in Which People Feel
    Deeply Recognized   89

Part Four: Paradoxes of Congregational Mission

8. Product and Process:
    Valuing Ends and Means Equally   105

9. Mission and Maintenance: Moving the
    Congregation Toward Achieving Its Goals While
    Fostering Goodwill and Group Cohesion   117

10. Conclusion: Leading Others to Double Vision   129

References   137

Index   139

Foreword

L eadership in religious organizations is not the same as that in corporations or government. Corporate and government leaders can find many books to help them become better leaders. Religious leaders, too, need a book on leadership they can call their very own. I believe *Living with Paradox* is that book. The word *paradox*, itself, points beyond our knowledge. In this book, Malony asks us to take the extra step to the area beyond what we know.

You may think that a book about paradox should have two forewords. Malony, however, asks leaders early on to move beyond the "either/or" concept to "both/and." And at his direction, we will settle for one foreword. He proposes a radical "double vision" approach to the paradoxes inherent in the life of the religious leader. Religious leaders, of course, do more than preach; they are a diverse group engaged in the mission and purposes of religious organizations.

For Malony, religious leadership differs from other kinds of leadership, because, as he states in Chapter Three, "Religion cushions life at the most profound level of fate, circumstance, change, tragedy, and meaning. When people are faced with frustration or tragedy, they are very vulnerable, and they overreact by confounding the roles of their leaders." Yet religious leaders, like other leaders, face real, pragmatic questions about the future of their organizations.

Living with Paradox contains stories, insights, questions, and sig-nals—even a few answers. It is clearly an expression of Malony's maturity, experience, and wisdom. Although he offers suggestions and directions, what you learn from this adult book is up to you. This is refreshing stuff because he helps us get through life without fooling ourselves. He asks us to grow up and get with it.

Among other things, he shows us that we have the opportunity to discover that living well with our paradoxes does not include try-ing to resolve them. Rather, we learn that living well with our para-doxes is both natural and also the best path to becoming effective leaders. But Malony is not concerned only with effectiveness. Faith-fulness in the teeth of ambiguity and complexity and antipathy lies also at the heart of true leadership.

The tensions inherent in a religious leader's job are confronted realistically and helpfully, as Malony uses a wonderful array of stories and examples to clarify his "double vision" premise. He offers great examples of how dialogue in a setting of respect lubricates organi-zations and enables high-potential relationships. The candor of his stories leaves us no place to hide. We're all in this book. This, of course, is one reason *Living with Paradox* is required reading.

As you read and think about this book, you are likely to muse, "After all these years, how come I don't know these things?"

This book does not simply teach you how to gain easy consen-sus. Rather, it points the way to a workable method of dealing with paradox, which makes it possible for adults to be accepting and effective even when they can't agree—for most of us, a quite nor-mal way of living and working. In the context of today's organiza-tional realities, Malony explains the uniqueness of the Christian calling when he says, "religious organizations are created to induce justice, mercy, and humility." With the help of this book, how these qualities can come to life in your organization ceases to be a mystery.

Newton Malony and I have been friends for thirty years. He has been one of my teachers, and we have taught courses together at

Fuller Theological Seminary. I know him well, and he knows what he is talking about. I commend to you the fidelity of his insights, his experience, and his wisdom.

February 1998   MAX DE PREE

Preface

. . . .

Religion is *big* business. Many congregations offer programs every day of the year and have annual budgets hovering near a million dollars. One denomination recently boasted that it has a church in every zip code in the nation. A recent survey of Americans found that 65 percent belong to some religious group.

Although scholars assert that religion is one of the three major institutions of every society—the other two being family and government—the fact is that religion is more like a business than a family. In long years of teaching church management, I have become convinced that in our society religion functions alongside other organizations that set goals, produce products, and market ideas. Religious organizations survive or fail according to the same rules that govern every business on every corner.

Furthermore, religious organizations, like secular organizations, can be developed. Religion shares all the blessings and banes of any human group in which people come together to accomplish goals. What is bad in groups can get worse; what is good can get better. Groups have lives of their own. They can be developed into organizations that fulfill the lives of their members at the same time that they produce products that sell on the open market.

I have written this book to reconstrue the role of religious leaders in management terms as they face what I consider to be the most critical aspect of their role, namely, the paradoxical nature of the religious environment. I am convinced that religious leaders who conceive of their roles in purely religious terms will never achieve full effectiveness. Furthermore, the ones who succeed best are those who face the paradoxes in their environment and attempt to live with the double truths they represent.

Of the treatises that I have written in an extended academic career, this is the one in which I have felt most invested and for which I have the highest hopes. The approaches to paradox that this book proposes are grounded in sound management theory. At the same time, the book acknowledges the unique aspects of the religious enterprise. If readers do in fact move from an "or" to an "and" style of leadership—if they develop the genius of double vision—then my goal will have been accomplished.

Acknowledgments

I am grateful to Sarah Polster for stimulating my thinking toward the writing of this book; to Sheryl Fullerton for her guidance; and to Lorraine Anderson for turning my ideas into readable English.

February 1998   H. NEWTON MALONY
                                                    Pasadena, California

The Author

H. NEWTON MALONY is senior professor in the Graduate School of Psychology of Fuller Theological Seminary, where he has taught since 1969. He is an ordained United Methodist minister and clinical psychologist, a Diplomate in Clinical and Forensic Psychology, and a Fellow of the American Psychological Association and the American Psychological Society. He is the author or editor of more than thirty books and the founding editor of the *International Journal for the Psychology of Religion*. Malony has a longtime interest in religious leadership, having taught church management and conflict management in Fuller Seminary's Doctor of Ministry program for more than fifteen years. Among his previous books are *Church Organization Development: Perspectives and Processes* (1985), *The Psychology of Religion for Ministry* (1996), and *The Psychology of Clergy* (1994).

1

Religious Leadership and Paradox

In the Harvard Business School case study "Walnut Avenue Church,"[1] the church's steeple was destroyed by lightning one stormy night. The church's pastor had no way of anticipating the gale of controversy that was about to whip through the congregation. The pastor immediately called an emergency meeting of the church's trustees the morning after the storm. At the meeting, the trustees decided to recommend to the congregation that the tower be capped to avoid further damage and that bids be invited from contractors for the rebuilding of the steeple over the next several months. The pastor agreed to announce this recommendation at worship services the next day.

Neither the pastor nor the trustees were prepared for the tumultuous debate that followed the pastor's announcement. Both the music and missions committees asked for immediate reconsideration of the expenditure, on the grounds that the money could be better spent on worship resources and services to the poor. The largest benefactor in the congregation promised to give a special donation toward the project—and threatened to leave the church if the steeple were not rebuilt. "Without a steeple, no one will know it's a church," he protested.

Although the pastor didn't realize it, he was faced with one of the perennial paradoxes embedded in religious leadership. All parties to the steeple debate at Walnut Avenue Church were expressing basic truths. Religious organizations, by their very nature, exist to stimulate worship and serve the poor; thus the requests of the music and missions committees were entirely reasonable. On the other hand, religious organizations have to have buildings in which to meet that are recognizable by their architecture and safe from storms, and thus the benefactor was right in his insistence that the steeple be rebuilt. Further, the trustees knew that the church could not exist for long with a steeple that let in wind and rain.

Paradoxes like these face leaders of religious organizations all the time. Indeed, paradox is the environment in which religious leaders routinely work. Thus, stepping into the role of religious leadership in these times can seem like suddenly grasping a live electrical wire—such is the shock of encountering the contradictions, incongruities, enigmas, quandaries, and perplexities that characterize the role. Religious leaders must be able to recognize and live with paradox if they're to be effective in the role.

A paradox is something that involves an inherent contradiction. More particularly, each of the paradoxes of religious leadership that we're about to explore consists of two propositions that are both essentially true but that appear to contradict each other. For example, the late Christian theologian Karl Barth posed a paradox in discussing evangelism. On the one hand, it seems obvious that people make a choice when they become religious. On the other hand, in some sense the choice has already been made for them. Both statements are true, but the ideas seem contradictory.

Barth was practical enough to know that in evangelism leaders have to work hard to convince individuals that accepting the Christian faith is a good choice for them. He knew that, in one sense, religion choice is no different from other important decisions people make in life. They think over the options and make the choice that best meets their needs at the time. In evangelism, people act when they determine that becoming Christian will meet their needs—and not before. Thus, religious conversions are based on conscious and voluntary choices.

At the same time, Barth was convinced that God chooses people rather than being chosen by them. In a theological sense, God "chose" human beings many centuries ago in creation and reaffirmed that choice in the life, death, and resurrection of Jesus Christ. When persons become Christians, then, they are not deciding to choose God; they are acknowledging that they have been chosen by him. Barth stated that there is no difference between persons inside the church and those outside: both have been chosen to be loved by God. But the people inside the church know it, while the people outside the church do not.

These opposite assertions about evangelism form a paradox. One truth is psychological: people choose God. The other is theological: God chooses people. The words of an anonymous hymn state this paradox in a lyrical fashion:

> I sought the Lord,
> and afterward I knew
> he moved my soul to seek him,
> seeking me.
> It was not I that found,
> O Savior true;
> no, I was found of thee. . . .
> I find, I walk, I love, but oh,
> the whole of love is but
> my answer Lord, to thee!
> For thou wert long beforehand
> with my soul;
> always thou lovest me.[2]

This paradox is an example of the types of seeming contradiction that surround religious leadership. Although every situation confronted by leaders everywhere has elements of paradox, leaders of religious groups are particularly confounded by just such predicaments. Why this is so has to do with the nature of the religious enterprise itself.

Religious leaders need to become mindful of the paradoxes that will plague their vocation in the years ahead. Paradoxes persist; they do not go away simply because we pretend they do not exist or choose to overlook one or the other of the truths they embody. Paradoxes can also be anticipated, understood, and acted upon. Increasing religious leaders' ability to live with paradox is the goal of this book. The task begins with such leaders' acknowledging that they live in a world where paradox is as pervasive as the air they breathe.

Why Paradox Is Central to the Religious Enterprise

Barth's understanding of evangelism is only one of many paradoxes that pervade the religious enterprise. Perhaps the central paradox is that religious organizations are based on otherworldly concerns and yet must function in this world. Such organizations, in the final analysis, are intended to "be everything, but do nothing," in the words of James Dittes, author of *The Church in the Way*. According to Dittes's conception, religion is that enterprise which ties together all the loose ends of life into a symphony of meaning and purpose.

All the great religions of the world consider insight into life's meaning and purpose to be a gift not based on anything that people do. In the Christian faith, there is the added conviction that the future is in the hands of a God who will accomplish his will for the universe quite apart from anything and everything that humans do. Religious leaders are, therefore, to be more concerned with being than with doing. And they are to lead in such a manner that those who follow them are willing to refocus their attention in the same way. Yet no organization that does nothing or offers no product to the market can stay in business for long. Religious organizations must both *do* something and *be* something—and therein lies a paradox.

Religious organizations are like other groups in many ways, but they are unique in their theological dimension, the one from which most of their paradoxes spring. Were space travelers to observe a school classroom, a congregational meeting, a Kiwanis Club luncheon, a Bible study group, a gathering of the telephone company's board of directors, and a group of Sierra Club members on a hike, they might conclude that these groups were all alike. In sociological terms, they all appear to be groups of people who have come together to accomplish a task or reach a goal. They all look like organizations, as organizations are defined in many textbooks. But beneath this apparent similarity, there is a distinct difference between those groups that are religious and those that are not: the religious groups have faith in a supernatural reality as a central ingredient. Most decisions in the religious groups are made following prayers that such decisions be attuned with God's will.

It is important for religious leaders to remind themselves frequently of this distinctive feature, as it affects almost every aspect of their functioning. In a lecture, Samuel Southard, a well-known teacher of pastoral counseling and a Presbyterian minister, illustrated the tendency to forget that faith is the basis of religious life. He stated that the first question he asks people when they come to him for counseling is, "Do you know where you are?" They readily answer, "Of course I know where I am; I'm in your office." Southard continues, "But do you know what this building is?" "It's a church," they answer. "Good," he replies; "please do not forget that. This is a church, not the counseling center down the street. This building has a steeple with a cross on it; I am a pastor, not a marriage and family counselor." Southard's next question is, "Do you expect me to keep what you share with me in confidence?" They answer without hesitation, "Of course I do." He then responds, "I have no intention of doing so." He shares with his counselees the paradox of the kind of counseling that goes on within the walls of a religious organization: "I am but the representative of the ministry of this church. All the members of our congregation are ministers. If I can think of a person in our congregation who has dealt with a problem such as yours, I will call them and tell them about your situation. I will urge them to get in touch with you. We are the church, and our help for persons is guided by II Timothy 1:7, which states, 'For God did not give us a spirit of cowardice, but rather a spirit of power and of love and of self-discipline.' "[3]

As is easily seen, this approach violates the presumed rule of confidentiality of counseling in favor of an approach based on a theological commitment to congregational ministry. This commitment, in turn, is grounded in a shared belief in a God who has become a part of the members' life, a God who intends that persons respond to him by helping others. There is a right to privacy in counseling, on the one hand. But on the other, there is the pastoral ministry of the church. It is the theological basis of church life that gives rise to this paradox, as it does to almost all of the other paradoxes detailed in this book.

Adopting the Paradoxical Mind-Set

It is important for religious leaders to remind themselves and their colleagues regularly of the theological basis of religious life. It is even more important for them to affirm and work with the paradoxes that necessarily arise from this foundation. This requires double vision. It asks leaders to move beyond "either/or" to "both/and." Either/or thinking asserts that paradoxes can be resolved by choosing one alternative over another. By contrast, both/and thinking embraces both sides of a paradox and asserts that each contains truth. To become a leader with double vision means, in the words of F. Scott Fitzgerald, "to hold two opposed ideas in the mind at the same time, and still retain the ability to function." He calls this a test of first-rate intelligence. I agree. It is also a test of first-rate religious leadership.

Living with paradox is a skill that can be learned. It is an essential skill, according to James Collins and Jerry Porras, authors of *Built to Last: Successful Habits of Visionary Companies*. In their comparison of highly successful companies with those that are only

mediocre, these authors find that every successful company has leaders who can live and work with paradox. These leaders have learned
the value of living with two seemingly contradictory forces or ideas
at the same time. They have ceased to use the either/or approach
and have become both/and leaders.

Rationally, it makes sense to be a single-vision leader—to identify opposing forces and move quickly to embrace one while denying the other, to make the hard decisions and enforce them. But
Collins and Porras suggest that either/or thinking can *tyrannize* a
company; leaders can be oppressed by thinking they always have to
choose one option to the exclusion of the other. It is the *genius* who
can see both sides of a paradox without becoming disoriented.
Geniuses have double vision. They can think paradoxically. They
can see both sides and can come up with novel and workable
options that respect both.

In describing what it means to be a both/and leader instead of
an either/or leader, Collins and Porras insist they are not talking
about *balance*. Balance implies compromise: a little of this and a little of that, fifty-fifty, half and half. Although negotiation and compromise may be called for at times, double-vision leadership implies
trying to value both sides of a paradox at the same time: being *both*
idealistic *and* profitable at the same time; *both* having a dominant
ideology *and* being open to change; doing very well in *both* the short
term *and* the long term. The Chinese cosmological symbol that
combines yin and yang is a good metaphor for this type of leadership. In the symbol, the black of the yin and the white of the yang
do not mix to form gray; both retain their purity but flow together
in a pattern that harmonizes the two sides.

Although the types of paradox with which religious leaders have
to deal may differ from those of commercial businesses, the skill of
double vision is of equal, if not more, importance for them. In the
example of Barth's evangelism paradox, neither side of the paradox
encompasses the whole truth. In evangelism, both human and
divine choice are involved. To affirm either the human or the

divine side of the paradox to the exclusion of the other would be to engage in denial and artificiality. It would lead evangelizers down a dead-end path.

Collins and Porras go so far as to say that companies that last, that will succeed in the future, have leaders who learn to live with paradox. This may be even more true for religious groups. Where paradoxes are noted and acknowledged, religious groups thrive. Where paradoxes are ignored or denied, religious groups may survive but they do not flourish. Thus, adopting the "paradoxical mind-set"—that is, developing double vision—becomes a primary skill for the effective religious leader. Although daily tasks may dominate consciousness, such leaders are able, just beneath the surface at the level of the subconscious, to sense the paradoxical nature of situations and to live through such situations with humility and courage.

Major Paradoxes of Religious Leadership

Forewarned is forearmed, according to the old maxim. If paradox is a central feature of religious life, then it is crucial to be able to describe in some detail the various paradoxes leaders might encounter. The remainder of this chapter names eight fundamental paradoxes of religious leadership; each following chapter takes up one paradox in depth. Each paradox embodies a challenge that is central to the religious leader's mission. But these eight paradoxes do not exhaust the list; there are others, and it behooves leaders to become prepared to see and deal with them. My hope is to evoke a general skill of paradox management through discussing these eight major paradoxes.

It is helpful to categorize the eight paradoxes under four general dimensions of religious organizations, as paradoxes of *role, perspective, structure,* and *mission.*

All leaders have *roles:* sets of behavioral expectations, both personal and group. Typically, religious leaders base their leadership pattern on some religious experience of their own. This experience leads to an inner sense that being a religious leader is what they ought to do. Thus, their authority is located both in personal life and in the tradition they attempt to serve. The expectations of the group are, as well, grounded both in group experiences and in traditional customs. These combinations provide fertile ground for the first two paradoxes: the person/position paradox and the prophet/priest/king paradox.

The *person/position paradox* pertains to how persons obviously enact the same role differently. On one side of the paradox, personal backgrounds, traits, and styles enhance or impede leadership acts. On the other side, all religious organizations delineate the responsibilities that go with leadership roles, and followers themselves react differently to various styles of leadership. The paradox is intensified by the sense that many expectations stem from an authoritative source: the Bible. There is another dimension to this paradox as well: all religious leaders live personal lives off the job (as the old saying goes, even Gods must eat!) but at the same time are expected, and may expect themselves, to give their total energy to the mission of the group.

The *prophet/priest/king paradox* involves the threefold roles that religious leaders traditionally assume when they take on the position of congregational minister. Too much or too little of any one role leaves leaders feeling their ministry is imbalanced. How leaders proclaim as prophets, comfort and console as priests, and govern as kings or queens is experienced in a somewhat confused and amalgamated manner by the members of their congregations. This leads to a significant paradoxical dimension of the leadership task that is not typical of secular settings.

Paradoxes of perspective pertain to the multiple concepts of the group experienced by leaders and followers. These paradoxes have to do mainly with the nature of religion and the roles of religion in the world as conceived by leaders and experienced by members. Both sociological and traditional influences are involved. How leaders manage these paradoxes leads to decisions regarding both time spent on and emphasis given to one of two possible orientations. Issues relating to perspective give rise to the inclusivity/exclusivity paradox and the timely/timeless paradox.

The *inclusivity/exclusivity paradox* refers to the line the religious leader walks between embracing all variations of faith and emphasizing the unique convictions of a particular denomination. To be too broad in defining which convictions are acceptable is to run the risk of violating the sociological truth that group cohesion and identity is based on beliefs that distinguish one group from another. On the other hand, to ignore basic similarities leads to lack of cooperation and denial that there are a number of fundamental areas of agreement across denominations and even among religions. Leaders walk a tightrope with their members as they manage the emphasis they put on each side of this paradox.

The *timely/timeless paradox* expresses the inevitable tension between the timeless truths of religion and the timely demands of a given historical period. Religion is, at one and the same time, conservative and revolutionary. Reinterpreting eternal truth in a way that leads to valid contemporary application has been called "the Protestant principle." No other leaders in our culture find it necessary to refer their ideas to ancient sources of authority like the Bible. For religious leaders, this becomes the basic theological task of exegesis (original intent) and exposition (present application). The perennial goal for religious leaders is to find God's will for a given situation.

The third type of paradox faced by religious leaders is *structural*. These paradoxes address the ways in which religious groups are organizationally unique. Although leaders share functions with other managers and executives across many types of groups, there are a number of structural features that make religious leadership different. The two paradoxes considered in the third section of the book are the for-profit/not-for-profit paradox and the person/organization paradox.

The *for-profit/not-for-profit paradox* applies to the financial side of religious organizations. Religious organizations often claim they are nonprofit, but (notwithstanding the sense that they are not amassing wealth) this claim is, in fact, not true. No organization lasts whose income does not exceed outgo—in money, energy, and time. In this sense, all religious organizations must show a "profit." Yet there is a deeper sense in which religious groups provide a "service without concern for cost" to the community. No commercial business would claim to do the same. The unique ways in which religious groups combine these concerns make for a dynamic paradox.

The *person/organization paradox* refers to how being part of an organization is experienced by leaders and followers. In thinking about religious organizations, we rarely conceive of leaders as "producers" and members as "consumers." Yet, that is what they are. Religious groups attempt to meet deeply felt personal needs, through programs that involve impersonal coordination of group effort. This paradox results in tensions that must be faced. Church members can feel lost in the midst of the very programs that are supposed to meet their deepest needs if the personal way in which these needs are experienced is not somehow honored by the organizational process.

Last, paradoxes in religious leadership can be related to the *mission* of the organization. Even though, like businesses in a market economy, religious institutions do have a market and they do have goals, they can never be viewed or understood in quite the same manner as nonreligious enterprises. Thus, although the two paradoxes to be described here—the product/process paradox and the mission/maintenance paradox—have counterparts in all organizational life, they nevertheless take on distinctive features when encased in a religious framework.

The *product/process paradox* addresses the relative importance of how a thing is done and the final product itself. Many participants in religious groups care less about what the group does and more about how people relate to each other in the process. Yet total emphasis on process can lead to failure to produce anything. A congregation offering no programs would not be a congregation. Such a congregation might *be* everything but *do* nothing. Nevertheless, in a paradoxical sense, members have expectations about interpersonal processes in religious groups that they do not apply to groups that are more secular. This dual perspective leads to perennial dilemmas in church life.

The *mission/maintenance paradox* is a variation on the product/process paradox. Leaders face the necessity to lead in a manner that advances organizational goals, and at the same time to apply their energies to cultivating good feelings within the group itself. It is widely recognized across the range of organizations that work groups in which there is inner conflict produce inferior products. This is no less true in religious groups. More important, interpersonal goodwill and cohesion are often considered to be as valid an index of "religiousness" as the funds that are given to the poor or the programs sponsored by the group. Thus, spending time maintaining the organization both gets in the way of, and yet is an essential conduit for, the mission. In another dimension of this paradox, leaders must never forget the tendency of members to resist change when things are going well. They prefer leaving things as they are and this often hinders advancement of the group's mission.

◆   ◆   ◆   ◆   ◆   ◆

Some time ago, the Harvard Business School published a book by Charles Handy titled *The Age of Paradox*. Handy put his finger on how important it is for leaders to learn to live and work in the midst of paradox. He was a prophet. If there is one theme to be reiterated about paradox, it is this: "Things haven't changed; things won't change; paradox is here to stay." The twenty-first century will only see paradox assume a greater importance than ever, especially for religious leaders.

The continuing centrality of paradox makes learning to manage it more significant than ever before. I hope the discussions in the following chapters enhance those skills, taking leaders from the tyranny of the *or* to the genius of the *and*.

Notes

1. "Walnut Avenue Church," 1973.

2. Anonymous, 1989, p. 341.

3. Public lecture by Samuel Southard, Vanderbilt University, 1963.

Part I

Paradoxes in the Religious Leader's Role

2

Person and Position
Being True to Oneself and to Congregational Expectations

Whenever parishioners get together and discuss present and past ministers who have served their congregations, the conversation gives some hint of the paradoxical tension between the person and the position. One individual says something like, "Our pastor is the best preacher we've had since Jim McDonald was here," and another chimes in, "If only she would visit the members, she would be the best minister we've had in a long time." Someone else might proclaim, "I really like the way our pastor relates to us on the committees; she sure knows how to make us feel needed." On a negative note, one bard said that his pastor had the "hoof and mouth" disease: "He can't preach and he won't visit."

The point is that every congregation has legitimate, well-tested, traditional role expectations for its leader, and at the same time each religious leader has his or her own style and priorities. As a result, no one person carries out perfectly all of the duties required by the position. The paradox is that leaders must serve both the truth of institutional expectations and the truth of their own personal history and approach.

This tension between the expectations of the role and the style of the leader exists in any organization. A military commander's office, for example, displays a large "Table of Order and Command" showing in bold letters all the titles of the various positions within the battalion. They range from battalion commander to motor pool sergeant. Beneath each is a slot that takes the name of the person occupying the position at a given time. As this system well indicates, persons change but positions do not; the position title is printed in permanent bold letters while the name of the person filling the position is on a piece of paper. The duties never change, but different persons fulfill them differently.

Although the tension between the person and the position made explicit in the military by the Table of Order and Command is implicit in all organizations, it becomes a serious paradox in religious leadership. This is due to the gravity of the functions that religious leaders perform. If we presume that religion is the way we handle fate, tragedy, and mystery in life, then it makes sense to say that no other leaders in our society deal with matters as serious as these. Of course, physicians and teachers deal with one or two of these realms, but religious leaders alone relate to people in all three. When people face these concerns their needs are deep-seated, and thus their expectations of religious leaders are high.

The fact that people have higher expectations of their minister than of secular leaders was illustrated by an incident involving church employment practices. The secretary of a church became pregnant and requested some time away after the birth of her baby. During the weeks she was on leave, the personnel committee decided to reconsider the secretarial needs of the church in light of budget problems it was having as well as the fact that the secretary and the pastor did not work well together. The committee decided to reduce the job from full-time to half-time. When they informed the secretary, at first she expressed interest in the part-time position but later declined their offer.

The secretary interpreted the change in job hours as the pastor's effort to get rid of her, and she complained to other church members about his "un-Christian" behavior. Demanding a public apology from him and a reinstatement to her former full-time job, she claimed that "this man of God acted like any secular, nonreligious boss out in the world; he showed no compassion for my situation."

Clearly, her expectations in this situation were higher than they would have been in a secular setting. Being fired or laid off in the secular world may provoke anger, but it does not usually provoke accusations of hypocrisy and lack of compassion.

Other unique aspects of the ministerial role bring the person/position paradox to the fore as well. Religious leaders serve a broader clientele than any other leaders in our culture: people of every age and station. First graders, college graduates, expectant mothers, auto mechanics, retired school teachers, dying octogenarians: all have expectations of their pastors. Further, there is no other work whose routine functions can be interrupted so easily by crises of sickness and death as that of the minister. Staying on well into the night to lend support in an hour of need is an unplanned-for disruption of the next day's activities. Religious leaders face this sort of thing week in, week out. These two factors add to the need for pastors to be extraordinarily flexible as they try to meet congregational expectations and also remain true to their own priorities and style.

Serving the Truth of the Self

A religious leader's interests, preferences, and style of leadership tend to spring from his or her personal history or life experience. More often than not, pastors feel "called" to do the work they do. Typically, this means they have experienced some sort of epiphany in which they felt set apart or chosen by God to be a religious leader. This experience—which, it should be noted, is usually not shared by those in secular leadership roles—can heavily influence what kind of leader a person is.

Religious callings can be of two kinds: natural or special. In a *natural* calling, one chooses to become a religious leader after a prayerful and rational self-analysis of one's own talents, interests, and skills. In a *special* calling, one chooses to become a religious leader after a mystical experience of being touched by God and selected to fulfill the role. More often than not, this special calling does not start with any sense that one is especially qualified to fulfill the role.

For example, Geoffrey felt both a natural and a special calling. He was a successful real estate broker when he accepted his pastor's invitation to become a member of the vestry in his church. He grew to look forward to the monthly meetings, and in his second year he was asked to head the buildings and grounds committee. He enjoyed the work and would often check in with the church maintenance staff on his way to the office. Sometime later, Geoffrey noticed a flyer about a spiritual growth retreat to be held at a nearby camp. When he told his wife about it, she agreed to go with him. At the retreat the leader challenged everyone to reflect on the meaning of their lives and to ask themselves if they were doing what God wanted them to do. Geoffrey took a long walk after supper and prayed about his life. When he returned, he told his wife that he had a strange feeling God wanted him to become a parish priest in the Episcopal church. She was surprised but said she would follow him wherever God led, and she encouraged him to sleep on it. In the weeks that followed, he still felt called to the role. So he soon closed his real estate business and attended seminary. He is now in his seventh year of ministry in a small town in Minnesota. If you asked him why he became a minister, he would reply, "Because God called me."

Both natural and special callings propel religious leaders into looking at what they do with a stronger sense of compulsion than any other leaders in our society. The truth of a pastor's individual calling is a powerful counterpart to the truth of the role expectations laid on her or him by the religious tradition. What is denigrated in a given leader's style, may, in fact, be a priority mandated by that person's sense of call.

The Theological School Inventory (TSI)[1], a scale used widely by seminaries as an entrance test and also used in psychological evaluations of ministerial candidacy, gives some sense of the different *motives* that lie behind the priorities that a particular religious leader might choose to emphasize in his or her ministry. The TSI scale identifies seven aspects of ministry and asks candidates to think about the relative importance of each of these motives in their decision to become a minister:

- Intellectual concern: study and teaching

- Self-fulfillment: prayer, meditation, spiritual and personal growth

- Leadership: direction of and vision for a local congregation

- Evangelistic outreach: convincing and converting people to religious faith

- Social reform: concerns for justice and ethical actions in the community

- Service to persons: help to the poor and less fortunate

- Acceptance by others: doing whatever one has succeeded at in the past as indicated by other people's responses; for example, if people have approved of a leader's work with youth, a leader might want to focus on youth ministry

A leader's priorities may stem from a sense of calling, but preferences for certain aspects of the job description develop over time and result from experiences in which a leader has been unusually successful. A scale called the Inventory of Religious Activities and Interests (IRAI)[2] helps leaders identify those religious *activities* that are particularly pleasing or satisfying to them. This scale measures interest in performing ten different religious roles:

1. Counselor: bringing comfort and encouragement to people and helping people solve personal problems

2. Administrator: planning, promoting, and executing congregational programs

3. Teacher: administering and teaching in the educational program of the congregation

4. Scholar: teaching at the college or seminary level in the field of religious studies

5. Evangelist: telling people about the beliefs of the faith and encouraging them to accept those convictions

6. Spiritual guide: assisting people in developing and deepening their religious faith

7. Preacher: preparing and delivering sermons and homilies

8. Reformer: speaking out against social and personal injustice and participating in programs for community betterment

9. Priest: leading liturgical and sacramental worship; performing sacred rituals

10. Musician: conducting and performing musical events in the congregation

Since, in most cases, religious leaders work long hours and never do everything that could be done, it is to be expected that they gravitate toward tasks that they find most satisfying and in which they have been most successful. The more interest a leader has in a given type of ministry, the more likely it is that she or he will put time and energy into that task. In the final analysis, pastors experience the person/position paradox most intensely when what they are interested in emphasizing in their ministry does not match what the congregation expects them to do. The closer the agreement between job expectations and personal preferences, the less tension this paradox evokes.

Serving Congregational Expectations

As one humorous story goes, there once was a church that fired its pastor year after year. No one seemed to be able to last longer than twelve months. Unexpectedly, as one particular pastor's first year came to a close the church officials made no move to dismiss him. Another year passed, and then another, with no effort to replace him. The pastor was very puzzled because of the church's history of one-year-long tenures. Finally, he asked the chairman of the board, "Why haven't you asked me to leave when none of the other ministers stayed beyond a year?" "Well, Pastor," the chairman replied, "we never wanted a minister here in the first place, and you're the nearest to nothing we've ever had."

If this story seems absurd, it's because no church has such minimal expectations of its pastor. Still, the story illustrates the truth that the pastors who fulfill congregational expectations are the ones who stay on year after year. The expectations about the leader's role held by members of a congregation are just as important and valid as the priorities stemming from the leader's own personal history. As mentioned earlier, these expectations tend to be high because religious leaders deal with matters that penetrate to the very core of life: security, self-esteem, the dilemmas of fate, the ravages of the passage of time, the mystery of death, the meaning of life. Basically, religious leaders are expected to function as a bridge between the mundane and the mysterious. Congregations build up expectations of this sort over generations, while individual members fashion expectations out of their own experiences.

Martin Luther once said that the true church exists where the gospel is preached and the sacraments are administered. But these two roles do not exhaust the requirements most churches have for their ministers. One denomination, for example, states that "the church is of God and will be preserved to the end of time, for the conduct of worship and the due administration of his Word and Sacraments, the maintenance of Christian fellowship and discipline, the edification of believers, and the conversion of the world." This tradition expects its leaders to maintain fellowship and discipline, educate its members, and engage in evangelism, all in addition to conducting worship and administering rituals.

Although this statement extends the list of role expectations considerably, the tasks of preaching and administering the sacraments probably still have major importance. (At least in Protestant Christianity, most religious leaders are primarily judged on their preaching.) Nevertheless, the list is longer than Luther envisioned. In fact, the roles noted in the denominational statement basically match those listed in the Inventory of Religious Activities and Interests, discussed earlier. Such roles as counselor, teacher, scholar, spiritual guide, musician, and social reformer simply elaborate on the edification of believers, the creation of fellowship, and the conversion of the world. Whereas in smaller congregations the leader might be expected to perform all these roles, larger churches might hire assistants to work with youth, do pastoral counseling, direct the choir, or engage in evangelism.

In actuality, most religious organizations require more than simple performance of these roles. The *way* in which tasks are to be done is an important dimension of the job description. One study of ministerial effectiveness compared the style expectations of religious leaders with those of their governing boards.[3] Not surprisingly, those ministers who were rated most effective were those whose style of leadership was in greatest accord with the preferences of the members of the church board. Style was defined in terms of the leader's preferences for acting unilaterally versus collaboratively, for working long hours on a few days each week versus shorter hours on many days, for following the board's directions versus questioning them, for preaching about money or not doing so, for having appointments made through the secretary versus doing so personally, and for acting independently as opposed to acting only on a mandate from the board.

In many cases, expectations about how ministers undertake their role go unstated. Furthermore, religious leaders themselves often do not realize their own style preferences until, and unless, someone calls them to their attention. Nevertheless, *how* leaders go about their tasks is frequently as important to the congregation as what they do.

It is also true that expectations held by individual members of the congregation may outweigh expectations held by the congregation as a whole when it comes to evaluating a pastor's performance. These more weighty expectations are usually in the realm of attention to people in times of crisis. A good, and true, illustration of this concerns a Methodist minister in a small Alabama city in the 1950s. The city was a hotbed of Ku Klux Klan activity. In fact, the chief of police was a Klansman, and the Klan had enough clout to rent the high school football stadium every month for a public rally. In light of this climate, the pastor's sermons on racial equality were not always well received by the congregation. Much of the South at that time was resisting integration, and many of his church members disagreed with his ideas that people should be treated as equals. Even citizens who did not approve of the Klan thought of this pastor as a troublemaker. They hoped that ignoring the Klan would make it go away.

The editor of the weekly newspaper was one of the church members who took strong exception to what his pastor advocated. He would write editorials criticizing the pastor after each of his sermons on racial equality. Still, he never asked the bishop to dismiss the pastor, and the pastor was reappointed year after year, serving for more than twelve years. When a reporter asked the editor why he didn't agitate for removal of the pastor, he replied, "Who, me? I would never do that. He's my pastor. The night my mother died, he was the first one there and the last one to leave."

The way this pastor related to people during the crises of their lives was more important to members of his congregation than his opinions about race relations. Admittedly, attention to people's personal problems is important for any leader in any organization. When bosses show kindness during stressful times, people appreciate it; but they do not expect it. We don't expect the bank manager to stay with us for half the night in times of crisis. But to a certain extent, we do expect acts of deep support and great kindness from our religious leaders. Even when we disagree with these leaders on other issues, the disagreement pales in importance when pastors go out of their way to comfort us while we experience disaster. People do not forget such acts of kindness.

Living with the Person/Position Paradox

How does one serve both the truth of the self and the truth of congregational expectations? Knowing that tensions between personal preferences and positional expectations are inevitable provides a basis for holding on to both sides of this paradox. It is important to realize that paradoxes must be lived with; they can never be fully resolved. Beyond that, one can choose to approach the paradox through negotiation or accommodation, even though neither approach causes the paradox to go away.

In the negotiation approach, ongoing communication between the pastor and the congregation about the tensions caused by the person/position paradox is central. The result of this communication should be that the paradox is normalized and expected. The place to start is in negotiating a job description. Since religious leaders work well over sixty hours per week and still leave tasks undone, it is imperative that some agreement be reached on where priorities should be placed. Religious leaders need to make clear from the very beginning of their tenure which roles they will undertake and which roles will assume priority whenever there are constraints of time. They need to resist any temptation to assume that things have been settled in the hiring interviews. At least the first six months should be spent in meetings to work out the mutual expectations of their work.

Two things should happen in these meetings. First, the officials and the congregational members should come to understand that the person/position paradox is normal—not only early in the new leader's tenure but all along. Statements should be made in public meetings, and members should be encouraged to give honest feedback regularly about how the new leader is doing. Second, there should be open, explicit interaction between the leader and officials regarding expectations. Good will should be assumed, but this should not cover up disagreements. These negotiations should become regular and systematic as time goes on. Both parties to the paradox should feel free to continue expressing tensions and agreements.

The accommodation approach to the person/position paradox is suggested by one of the two main theories of leadership, the "credit" theory. Before discussing this theory, allow me to draw a contrast with the other, the "honeymoon" theory of leadership. The honeymoon theory suggests that leaders never have more power to exert their influence without evoking resistance than they have on their first day on the job. Like many marriage partners, leaders and followers may be happiest together early in the relationship. Leaders who adopt the "honeymoon" theory act quickly and decisively to exert their own personal priorities, styles, and preferences early in their tenure because they know that resistance to their leadership builds up over time and their power diminishes. They are aware that later on, their motivations will be questioned, their actions misperceived, and their words misinterpreted.

Unfortunately, the honeymoon approach treats the person/position paradox as if it can be ignored by totally emphasizing the leader's own personal priorities, styles, and preferences. It certainly doesn't represent a both/and approach. In contrast, the credit theory suggests a way to accommodate both sides of the paradox over time.

The credit theory implies that leaders have no power at the beginning of their tenures. As they carry out their duties, leaders build up credit in their leadership savings account by closely following organizational expectations. After some time, they have enough leadership credit in the bank so that they can diverge from expectations and help groups try things that they have never done before. From this point of view, the power to lead is not something leaders have but something followers give, as in the case of the newspaper editor who warmly appreciated the pastor whose political opinions he disagreed with. Another way to state this is that leaders earn their power; they do not deserve it just by virtue of their title. Influence builds up over time as members come to appreciate how leaders help them across the chasms of their lives. Only by waiting until they have leadership credit to spend can leaders truly effect significant change.

Following the credit theory, leaders live with the person/position paradox by accommodating themselves to traditional expectations at the beginning. They help the group do what it feels is important, in order to gain trust and lead the group into doing what the leader feels is important. When the leader has built up leadership credit, he or she can spend it by acting idiosyncratically. Then people will follow their styles, their priorities, and their preferences. I do not know whether the Southern pastor ever got the editor to change his mind about race relations, but the pastor definitely had built up leadership credit that he could spend without completely losing the editor's support.

Approaching the person/position paradox either through negotiation or accommodation, religious leaders can serve the truths of both their own personal histories and the expectations of their congregation. Either approach is a dynamic process that unfolds over time. Congregational members and officials come and go. Circumstances change. Individuals experience both triumphs and disasters. Although churches, like military battalions, have positions that must be filled, the organization itself is forever fluid. Thus, negotiation and accommodation must become a constant practice and can never be expected to resolve the person/position paradox once and for all.

Notes

1. More information about the Theological School Inventory can be obtained by writing to H. Newton Malony, Fuller Theological Seminary, 180 North Oakland, Pasadena, CA 91101.

2. More information about the Inventory of Religious Activities and Interests can be obtained by writing to Richard Hunt, Senior Professor of Psychology, Fuller Theological Seminary, 180 North Oakland, Pasadena, CA 91101.

3. Lichtman, 1987.

3

Prophet, Priest, and King

Playing Three Roles That Become Confounded

In the previous chapter, we examined a paradox related to religious leadership preferences and styles: that one naturally tends to emphasize certain roles at the same time one tries to meet congregational expectations. This chapter considers a second role-related paradox: that while the key roles of prophet, priest, and king are performed separately and each demands different skills, the congregation doesn't make these distinctions in evaluating a pastor's performance. In fact, the congregation inevitably confounds these roles. The task of religious leaders is to balance the truth that they must function in specific ways within certain roles with the truth that their performance is not differentiated, but is combined, in the minds of their congregations.

One parishioner's response to how a pastor carried out the kingly role illustrates the truth of this role confounding. In this case, friends gave money to buy an elaborate candelabra in memory of the parishioner's wife when she died. The church's worship committee, accepting the candelabra with appreciation, decided to use the gift only on special occasions. Because the pastor had been very attentive and close to this man during his wife's terminal illness, he was very hurt that the pastor did not sway the committee to vote to use the candelabra every Sunday. As he said to a friend, "He knew Gertrude well. Doesn't he know how much it would mean to me to see that candelabra standing up by the altar every Sunday during worship? Why did he forget and not speak up? I never thought he would give in to those on the committee who didn't know Gertrude." This church member expected the pastor to represent his wishes when he took off the hat of "priest" (providing compassionate understanding) and put on the hat of "king" (providing democratic leadership).

It's important to note that this paradox is about role *confounding*, not role *confusion* or *conflict*. The issue is not the problem that religious leaders have in confusing one role with another. Nor is it the problem of filling one role well and being inadequate in another, as when members say, "She's a good preacher but a lousy administrator." It's not even the problem of an overarching style interfering with one role or another, as in "He has a good bedside manner; we just wish he weren't so relaxed in leading the worship service." Instead, the issue is the tendency for members of religious organizations to intermix their perceptions of leaders into a composite, to fail to discern the differences between the key roles leaders perform—that is, to confound the roles.

Overtly, church members can make logical distinctions about their leader's performance in the three roles of prophet, priest, and king (or queen). But subconsciously, a general impression of the leader takes over, based on his or her performance in just one of the roles. Why this confounding occurs has to do with the deeply serious nature of the religious enterprise, as is the case with so many of the paradoxes examined in this book.

The Reality of Separate Roles

The three roles of prophet, priest, and king embody the classic set of duties for religious leaders. There is a long-standing expectation that leaders within the Christian tradition will fill these three roles. Although congregants can be expected to confound them, pastors must keep the roles separate and act appropriately in each.

As *prophets*, religious leaders fulfill the role of righteous judge. They speak for God. What they say about the religious meaning of life supposedly reflects God's evaluation of the affairs of the day. Religious leaders declare the wisdom of God about the times and circumstances of daily life. They preach sermons that reflect their prayerful judgment about sin, redemption, and grace. They call people to listen to God and follow God's direction. Phillip Brooks, the famous Boston cleric, was queried by one of his members as he walked into church one Sunday, "Got a fresh message from God for us this morning, Pastor?" The member was referring to Brooks's prophetic role.

This is an extremely demanding role. No other leaders in Western culture have the responsibility of speaking to the total membership of their organizations on a weekly basis. Yet sermons come every seven days in the life of the typical religious leader. Congregants expect profundity. They look for wisdom and guidance. They want entertainment, and they delight in good stories. They appreciate being noticed and talked about, but they don't want to be embarrassed. Speaking before a cradle-to-grave audience whose life experience is immensely varied is a perilous task, yet if people were asked to judge the effectiveness of their religious leaders on one single criterion, my guess is that most of them would choose the sermon as that yardstick.

As *priests*, ministers fulfill the role of compassionate servant. They declare the blessing of God on the events of daily life. They are present in times of sickness and death. They bury the dead, marry lovers, baptize infants, bless homes. They lead worship, celebrate sacraments, and proclaim truths about God's presence and care through the stages of individual and family life. They speak of God's love, guidance, and tender care for each and every one. The pastor of Wesley Memorial Church in Oxford, England, baptizes an infant and then "walks the church" with the baby held high so all can see, repeating as he does so a declaration that this is a child of

God whose care is now the responsibility of all in the church. As adoring parents look on and tears cloud the eyes of those who watch this spectacle, the minister is performing his priestly role.

As *kings*, pastors fulfill the role of benevolent ruler. They run the church. They govern. They share visions, inspire commitment, plan programs, and cultivate participation. They make decisions about money, property, and events. They oversee activities. They sit on committees, offer opinions, and make final decisions. They lead the organization.

In opening Chapter One, I drew on a Harvard Business School case study called "Walnut Avenue Church." The first in a series of publications by the Harvard Business School created for use in training ministers in how to lead their congregations, the case study focuses on how a pastor functions in the kingly role in the event of a crisis. Discovering the destruction of the steeple by lightning, the pastor calls the chairman of the board of trustees to report his discovery and then later meets with the trustees to decide whether or how to repair the damage. In this case the pastor is functioning in his governing role of keeping the buildings in good repair.

Although members of religious organizations know the difference between words spoken in a committee meeting and words uttered in a sermon, they expect an underlying consistency across roles that is, from one point of view, unrealistic. For instance, it's realistic to expect the pastor to give personal attention to members in the priestly role, but not in the kingly or prophetic role. Yet while everyone knows that their minister can't always treat them with warmth and support, they still expect it, because that is what God would do—and after all, the minister is a representative of God.

The Inevitability of Role Confounding

Inevitably, what religious leaders do in one role becomes entangled in their followers' minds with expectations about what they should do in the other roles. Confounding resulting from how leaders perform their priestly role is common. As representatives of the Christian God, whose name is *love*, pastors in their priestly role provide reassurance and support when illness or tragedy strikes. Parishioners who expect the same level of reassurance and support from the pastor in the kingly role are inevitably disappointed, as was the church member who wanted the candelabra used every Sunday in memory of his wife.

Another aspect of role confounding in the case of the priestly role occurs when parishioners generalize their hurt or appreciation regarding what a pastor does in this role to their evaluation of the pastor's performance as a whole. A common maxim among religious leaders is that "a lot of my members get sick, go to the hospital, go home, and get mad before I even know they are ill." Those who get mad presumably feel that the pastor isn't doing his or her job adequately.

Confounding can also spring from how leaders perform their prophetic role. It's no surprise that much role confounding results from what is said from the pulpit. A clear example of this kind of confounding occurred in the case of a pastor who was an excellent preacher. His insights were penetrating. He interpreted daily events with a wisdom that was unsurpassed. Most members of his congregation looked forward to his messages and found new understandings of how to apply their faith to their daily lives almost every Sunday. Furthermore, his priestly performance was always good. He could hold a funeral that left few eyes dry, and he seemed to know just what to say on every occasion. Few members could remember when he missed a sick bed. Yet in his kingly role he unintentionally offended one of his faithful supporters, and her support for him in his other roles was strongly shaken because she felt that he didn't practice what he preached.

The offense resulted from the pastor's altering the order of worship for the "Easter vigil" service held the night before Easter Sunday. Acting in his kingly role, the pastor decided to put the hymn "Up from the Grave He Arose" at the end of the service rather than at the beginning, because in his judgment this sequence made better sense. What he didn't realize—because he had only been at the church for ten months—was that one of the church members had initiated the vigil service herself after visiting her sister-in-law's church, where this kind of celebration was a beautiful, long-standing tradition. Using the order of worship from the other church, this faithful supporter had been in charge of the service for several years. The pastor didn't consult her in making the change because he was unaware of this history, and she didn't find out about the change until she picked up the bulletin on the afternoon of the service.

Because the pastor preached caring and concern for the feelings of others in his sermons, this church member couldn't understand his failure to consult her. She was so hurt and mad at the pastor that she could hardly participate in the vigil service. Although they talked afterward and he apologized, she harbored her hurt and began to miss morning worship services. When she had to go to the hospital for an operation, she told her husband she didn't want the pastor to visit her. She had confounded his performance in his kingly role with his effectiveness in his prophetic and priestly roles.

In this case, the pastor was simply exercising his duty as the leader in charge of worship at the church. I doubt that this church member would object, in principle, to the authority and obligation of the pastor to play this role. She fully expected him to have the bulletins ready, the heat on in the sanctuary, the ushers prepared, and the choir assembled. However, all of her normal expectations for how the pastor should act in his kingly role were forgotten when she discovered the change in "her" order of service. Then she evaluated his performance much more critically in light of his prophetic role.

In another variation on role confounding, church members can overlook or rationalize unsatisfactory performance in one role if they are impressed with performance in another. One church member presented to the church council a petition for a vote of "no confidence" in the senior pastor. During the discussion that followed, several people noted that the pastor seemed to be preaching the same sermons they had heard him preach three years ago. Others claimed his sermons were not as Bible-based as they used to be. At this point, an older man stood and gave an impassioned plea in favor of the pastor. He admitted that the sermons needed improvement but spoke plaintively about the pastor staying with him at the hospital when his wife had a serious operation several months earlier. A chorus of persons followed with testimonies about how the pastor had helped them during some crisis or supported them when they tried to get a mission project started. Reaction to the pastor's prophetic preaching was colored by feelings about his priestly ministrations during family crises, and his kingly support when the organizational structure needed changing.

After reading these examples, some may query, "But doesn't this happen in other, nonreligious organizations as well? Isn't it true that other leaders function in multiple roles that also become confounded in the minds of their followers?" My answer is an unequivocal no—at least, not to the same degree. Why this is so has to do with the high expectations that people have regarding religion, as discussed in Chapter Two. To reiterate, religion, more than any other institution in society, deals with deeply subjective and personal issues of existence. Religion cushions life at the most profound level of fate, circumstance, change, tragedy, and meaning. When people are faced with frustration or tragedy, they are very vulnerable, and they overreact by confounding the roles of their leaders.

According to University of Haifa psychologist of religion Benjamin Beit-Hallahmi, religious experience is necessary because life is so frustrating and stressful. Religion offers relief from distress by providing experiences that lift people above the reality of everyday life. Here they gain rest and renewal to return to the strain of daily living. Sociologist Peter Berger echoed this observation in his contention that the reason religion has not disappeared, as Freud and others have predicted, is that life has "black holes" that would be overwhelming were it not for faith. According to the late theologian

Paul Tillich, life poses the questions to which faith is the answer—and the answer always comes from outside life's situation, in the form of revelation. Although they did not use the same terminology, Beit-Hallahmi, Berger, and Tillich all reached the same conclusion: religious behavior is desperate behavior.

Thus, people have high expectations of religion. They look for wisdom on how to live, delivered by their pastors in the prophetic role. They look for compassion and guidance in the face of change, administered by their pastors in the priestly role. And they look for love and gentleness in the way the organization functions; they expect to be handled with care by their leaders in the kingly or queenly role. Because they assume that their religious leaders can see their needs and will meet them, they don't clearly separate these roles.

This confounding of the roles of prophet, priest, and king may also be inevitable because of the normative character of religious organizations—that is, the fact that participation is based on identification with the norms or principles for which religion stands. People aren't forced to join, as they are in coercive organizations such as public schools and the armed services. Nor are they paid or rewarded for participating, as they are in utilitarian organizations such as businesses or clubs. Although "hellfire and damnation" preaching still exists, involvement in most religious organizations is no longer based on the threat of punishment in an afterlife and thus is not coercive. And though some involvement in religion seems to be utilitarian—people expect prayers to be answered, and they derive identity and meaning from their involvement—there is no material payoff for being religious.

This distinction among normative, coercive, and utilitarian organizations has been made by the sociologist Amitai Etzioni and is helpful when we attempt to understand the role confounding that goes on in response to religious leadership. The woman who was upset over the change in the Easter vigil worship service reacted "normatively" to the experience. She perceived that her pastor had violated the norms or ideals that were basic to her participation. Had her congregation been a coercive organization, she would have felt she could say nothing. She would have continued to attend worship without complaining. Had her congregation been utilitarian, she might have felt offended but said nothing because her pay might have been reduced or she might have been fired for insubordination. But hers was a normative organization. Complain, she did. Confound the pastor's roles, she did. Withdraw her involvement, she did!

Living with the Prophet/Priest/King Paradox

Living with the prophet/priest/king paradox is similar to living life as a beekeeper. Regardless of what one does, one will inevitably get stung someday. Although religious leaders expect members of their congregations to know when they are functioning in one role and when in another, role confounding in religious organizations is inevitable and should be expected. It is wise for leaders to remember this certainty at the same time that they undertake measures to moderate the impact of role confounding.

This impact can be seen in cantankerous resistance or idealized conformity to the leader's ideas, depending on whether he or she has frustrated or satisfied the personal needs of the member. For instance, a parishioner who was comforted by the minister while in the hospital may well become uncritically accepting of the minister's ideas about how church services should be run. Thus, ministers must be much more vigilant than their secular counterparts in reflecting on what lies behind the ease or difficulty they experience in getting support for their ideas. When someone always opposes them or affirms everything they suggest, they should suspect that role confounding might be occurring.

Although it is impossible to achieve all the time, religious leaders should remain "program neutral" as much as they can in order to minimize role confounding. This means that they should seldom make known their ideas about what the congregation should do; instead, they should let the members of the congregation decide for themselves. Better decisions result, because the congregation doesn't become too leader dependent. Further, the chances that support, or lack of it, is due to overidealization or reactions to hurt are lessened.

Aside from this, leaders should consciously acknowledge the truth of both sides of this paradox. The roles of prophet, priest, and king are separate and distinct, but it is also true that people generalize or confound their impressions of leaders across roles, particularly in religious groups where they are dealing with such important issues in their lives. Leaders who complain when confounding happens or try to logically defend all their behavior are denying reality and get nowhere. They either spend all their time going around putting out the fires of negative feelings among their parishioners or they gravitate toward too-close friendships with their supporters. Both approaches are unwise. Thus, acknowledging the inevitability of role confounding is the first step in living with this paradox.

Making evaluation of their performance legitimate is the next step. Most religious leaders have been trained to get feedback, but very few have taken their training seriously. This lack of attention to how people are responding is very understandable. The acid that eats at most voluntary organizations (of which religious groups are examples) is *time*. There is never enough time to adequately plan and execute decisions. Things are always rushed, and immediately after one event ends there is another waiting to be planned. Add to this the natural tendency for leaders to be fearful of what people might say if they were given a chance, and it may seem better to just assume that everybody liked a program than to spend time evaluating it.

Although resistance to evaluation is widespread, the fact remains that everyone does it, leaders included. Moreover, evaluation is good. It should be encouraged. Some have interpreted God's directive to Adam and Eve in Genesis 1:28 to "have dominion and subdue the earth" as a mandate to have an opinion about life. This conclusion could be correct if, as some theologians have asserted, the frontal lobe of the brain is the locus of the image of God in human beings. We have the brain power, and possibly the obligation, to evaluate life and respond to it. Thus, religious leaders must make evaluation legitimate. Honor it. Plan for it. Expect it. Listen to it. Use it. Do not defend against it. Respond to it.

A final necessity is for religious leaders to try to be as considerate, consistent, and sensitive as they can be across the several roles that they play. Although leaders are human and often fail in these qualities, *intentional* reflection should become a rule. Intentional religious leaders, while recognizing imperfections in themselves and followers alike, spend significant time thinking through how they do what they do. Intentional religious leaders aim to be clear channels of the divine for those who follow them. They take seriously the feedback they get. They try to profit from evaluation. They hope for some consistency in their behavior but do not become immobile when they fail. They are willing to be courageous in making hard decisions, but they are also willing to apologize when that is called for.

Whereas role paradoxes pertain more to what a religious leader does, perspective paradoxes, to which we now turn, refer to approach and style.

Part II

Paradoxes of *Perspective*

4

Inclusivity and Exclusivity

Appreciating Both Uniqueness and
Universality in Faith Convictions

A number of American denominations have been dialoguing for more than two decades about the possibility of joining together in one united church. Known as the Consultation on Church Union (COCU), the movement was stimulated by similar efforts in such countries as India (the United Church of South India), Australia (the Uniting Church of Australia), and China (the Three Self Church). Many issues have been debated long and hard. For example, in a united church, will the Episcopalians recognize the ordination of the Baptists as legitimate for serving the Holy Communion, and will the Baptists recognize that sprinkling is as valid as immersion for the rite of baptism?

What is significant about this dialogue is that it is taking place over the Internet, far from the concrete reality of churches in neighborhoods ranging from upper Manhattan in New York City to the suburbs of Lincoln, Nebraska. Leaders on all sides of the issues have been sending e-mail messages to each other at an astounding tempo. The old question "Will it sell in Peoria?" is one somebody should be asking—and the answer is, "Probably not!" The members of most local churches are not giving a second thought, much less a first one, to combining with other churches in their communities. They would be surprised—even appalled—to know that their ministers are involved in conversations that might lead to the loss of their denomination's distinctive beliefs and practices.

The paradox is this: even though most religions are inclusive in that they share faith in a supernatural and idealist view of life, they are exclusive in believing that as a denomination they possess some perspectives on this issue that are unique and absolutely valid. Religious leaders might readily acknowledge that they share many convictions with leaders of other denominations, but at the same time they should realize that the members of their churches are not very interested in such commonalities. They should know that their members would probably be upset if they thought there were any chance the leaders did not share their strong allegiance to special beliefs and unique traditions. The task of religious leaders is to affirm the inclusive truth of the commonality they share with other religionists in a manner that does not violate another truth: that people choose and remain loyal to groups largely on the basis of the conviction that they share an exclusive and unique perspective.

The need to address this paradox is just one more example of how religious organizations differ from business organizations. Whereas religious leaders must be careful about admitting similarities in their positions or products, business executives don't hesitate to buy out another company if they think it will lead to increased profits. Employees might be concerned about losing their jobs, but questions about the loss of the bought-out company's unique way of doing business or special product line rarely trouble them or their leaders. If Sears Roebuck were to take over a Macy's store, the counters would be stocked the next day with products with both Sears and Macy's labels. The value of these products would be touted by the erstwhile Macy's employees with the same convictions asserted the day before.

The difference between businesses and religious groups lies not only in the fact that one is a utilitarian organization and the other is voluntary, as discussed in Chapter Three. Company workers worry about being fired, while the members of most congregations have the power to fire their bosses. Except in those parachurch organizations where members are there because it is a job, participants in religious groups quickly express their disapproval of leaders by using their pocketbooks or their feet: they quit giving or they quit attending. They also have formal power, because leaders in almost all religious organizations are subject to a congregational vote of confidence at the annual meeting. Thus, religious leaders must approach the inclusivity/exclusivity paradox cautiously or risk losing the attendance or confidence of their followers.

Trends in Church Membership: Inclusive Versus Exclusive Churches

A look at trends in church membership bears this out. In a book written in 1977, *Why Conservative Churches Are Growing*, Dean Kelley stressed the point that high-demand, firmly convicted, strong-doctrine churches were growing while overly inclusive, broad-belief, difference-embracing groups were losing members. Kelley's book states a basic sociological fact: people typically define their identity in terms of how they are different from others. For many, if not most, members of religious groups, it is anxiety provoking to suggest that they give up their unique convictions and embrace the legitimacy of those with whom they thought they disagreed. At the time that Kelley was writing, many conservative churches were reacting against the move by more liberal churches to come together "in spite of" their differences. The conservative churches that emphasized their distinctive beliefs were growing because they responded to people's need to be different.

Changes at the Worldwide Church of God plainly illustrate this trend. For many years this religious group advocated giving 20 percent of one's income to the church, based on the commands of the Bible as interpreted by the late Herbert W. Armstrong, the church's founder. Armstrong's successor, however, decided that his reading of the Scriptures revealed that tithing should be voluntary, not obligatory. Soon after he announced this to the members, the finances of the church plummeted. Whereas previously the church had been able to build a beautiful headquarters complex in Pasadena, California, operate a world-class performance auditorium, and support an undergraduate college, it soon had to scale back its operations and sell its property. Further, when the leaders extended the changes to desist engaging in a number of other behaviors that had typified their uniqueness, such as Saturday worship and nonassociation with unbelievers, the church's membership, as well as its finances, began to wane.

A rump group of pastors withdrew and reorganized themselves into a new church that retained all the old behavioral demands that had been declared null and void. Even though a number of them might have agreed with the new interpretations of the biblical prescriptions, they seemed to know that once the church became like all other churches, the attraction it had enjoyed would fade. The new group's membership increased while the mother church dwindled away. One wonders whether the loss of membership in the major denominations of the United States coupled with the increase in membership of a number of smaller, high-demand groups could not be explained in the same way as the changes of membership in the Worldwide Church of God.

The anxiety over membership and finances experienced by inclusive religious groups has no doubt provoked much thoughtful reflection. A prime thesis used by mainline denominational leaders to explain their loss of membership has been the "high religion/low religion" approach. This approach characterizes "low religion" as catering to people's need for certainty and authoritative answers, and "high religion" as trusting people not to need the security of "we-they" distinctiveness. High religion (which term characterizes mainline denominations as opposed to more conservative or fundamentalist groups) lacks the popular appeal of low religion. High religionists tend to ignore self-centered reasons for religion and, like the eighth-century prophet Amos, emphasize what they are called to do on behalf of others. They take pride in how much sacrifice such an approach requires and aren't surprised that only a few decide to follow them. They appear satisfied to lose members.

From this point of view, "fundamentalism" is received as more of an enemy than "secularism." At one recent alumni gathering of the Yale Divinity School, the featured preacher mentioned the evils of fundamentalism twenty times and failed to address the dangers of secularism even once. Still, the facts of church membership speak for themselves: it would be more profitable for religious leaders to spend their reflection on the dilemmas of the inclusivity/exclusivity paradox and plan their leadership around proven sociological facts.

Recognizing the Commonality Among Religious Groups

There are, indeed, many important issues on which the views of different religious groups are very similar. For example, they all tout the values of family, honesty, trustworthiness, peace, neighborliness, and hard work. In many communities, all denominations unite in evangelistic rallies, blood drives, children's services, and crime-reduction efforts.

This is perhaps particularly apparent to those religious leaders who have had graduate theological training. Along with their seminary professors, they realize that although they live in a pluralistic world replete with various beliefs, they share foundational convictions with those whom they appear on the surface to disagree with. Sometimes the foundational convictions that cross denominational lines motivate religious leaders to want to undertake cooperative efforts with other churches, although they may hesitate because they fear repercussions among denomination members.

On occasion, joining together across denominational differences may be the right thing to do no matter what the cost. Religious leaders may be convinced that a given societal tradition is wrong and needs attention regardless of whether their members agree or not. For example, in the 1950s ministers from numerous denominations in the southeastern United States met clandestinely to consider ways in which they could encourage their churches to accept people of all races. This was during a time when many church members were convinced that association with other races was wrong because it might lead to intermarriage—behavior that they considered to be sinful. These ministers attempted to be cautious by meeting some distance away from their churches, on black college campuses, but the state highway patrol often took down license numbers and thus found out the names of those who attended the meetings. By the time the ministers returned home, many in their congregations knew where they had been. In this case, the ministers knew that they differed radically from their congregations on an issue, but they felt the matter was important enough to take the risk that their inclusiveness would become known.

Seminaries have long been sensitive to the fact that they probably deal more reflectively with religious convictions than do most local church members. As their scholars study the religious environment of the ancient Near East during testamental times or engage in historical-critical studies of the Scriptures, they often consider hypotheses that would appear heretical to the average parishioner. Most seminaries are very cautious about the way they communicate these ideas to churches. In fact, it is well known that scholars speak one language to their academic colleagues and another to the general public.

This is no different from the practices of scholars in most fields, but the suspicion that is aroused by such a practice is more inflammatory in religion. This became clear in the Southern Baptist denomination in the 1960s and 1970s. Pastors became highly suspicious of seminary scholars during these decades and, in fact, sought in a number of cases to gain control over the seminaries and fire teachers they considered heretical. This resulted in some tragic changes in seminary education. It illustrates how easy it is for religious leaders to become embroiled in the inclusivity/exclusivity paradox.

There is real value in leaders' recognizing the common concerns they share with other religious groups. Competition may be healthy in many ways, but much good can be accomplished when churches join together and affirm similar priorities. The uniting of downtown churches in Pasadena, California, to build a center for homeless persons is a good example of an inclusive project that accomplished what no one of the churches could have accomplished by itself. The key to valuing both sides of the inclusivity/exclusivity paradox may be to accept exclusive independence at the neighborhood level but promote inclusive cooperation at the city, state, or national level.

Acknowledging Church Members' Need for Differentiation

Even though the search for commonality among congregations may be a noble one, the fact remains that people join particular religious groups *because of* their distinctive beliefs and practices rather than in spite of them. Comparisons help people feel stronger and more firmly positioned in the social world, as illustrated by the words of the Pharisee in the parable of the Pharisee and the tax collector (Luke 18:9–14): "God, I thank you that I am not like other men." Most persons glean their identity by such differentiations, be they in terms of clothes, achievements, habits, beliefs, or possessions. Their understanding of the groups to which they belong is based, to a great degree, on how they are different from other groups.

In addition to the sociological fact that groups are formed on the basis of differences that become the cementing truths holding congregations together, there is the psychological fact that most members of religious groups don't see their convictions as opinions. They aren't postmodernists who are cultural relativists. They see their religious beliefs as absolute, undebatable "truths." When these truths are challenged by inclusive ideas—by the suggestion that they might embrace beliefs and practices different from their own because there is in fact an underlying commonality—these church members rise up in defense. They interpret inclusiveness or doubts about the absolute rightness of their beliefs as threats.

Beit-Hallahmi has written about the "truth-value" of religious beliefs in an article called "Religion as Art and Identity." He contends that religion is like art in that both are ways of standing off to the side of everyday life and transcending it through acts of imagination, fantasy, and illusion. *Illusion,* as used by Beit-Hallahmi, does not mean the same thing as *delusion.* Delusions are beliefs that are untrue, whereas illusions are beliefs that could be true. From a psychological point of view, religion and art always go beyond empirical fact and are acts of creative imagination; they are interpretations of empirical reality. Religious ritual, religious worship, religious reading, religious action: all are acts of creative imagination, as are pieces of musical, dramatic, and literary art.

Both religion and art, from Beit-Hallahmi's point of view, are absolutely necessary for life, because (as we indicated in regard to his thesis on the function of religion in Chapter Three) they provide release and relief from the mundane, stress-filled events of people's daily lives. Existence is rough and raw without the alleviation that art and religion provide. Art and religion give people the respite that they need to return to everyday life with new verve, meaning, energy, and purpose.

But religion and art differ in one important respect, suggests Beit-Hallahmi. We know art to be a personal interpretation of some subject, which never pretends to approach photographic objectivity. By contrast, members of congregations don't consider their religious beliefs to be a personal interpretation of reality, but rather rock-solid truth. Religious persons believe in the truth-value of their convictions. Outsiders to given religious beliefs may look upon art and religion as the same—cultural and personal interpretations of life—but insiders make a radical distinction. In their minds, their convictions are not just personal opinions or the tenets of a cultural tradition; on the contrary, they are truths.

This distinction is well illustrated in the Roman Catholic Mass. Vivaldi's *Gloria* is an elaborately beautiful work of musical art that leads up to the blessing of the host in the ritual of the Mass. Parishioners can appreciate (and have done so for more than two hundred years) the *Gloria* as an act of creative imagination that evokes the prayerful state appropriate to what follows in the mass. On the other hand, throughout those two centuries, the church has persisted in asserting that in the elevation of the Host that follows the *Gloria*, the bread and wine become, in substantive actuality, the body and blood of Jesus Christ. This transformation is believed to be actual, not just a flight of creative imagination.

Myth is the term scholars apply to these beliefs, which vary from religion to religion. In the truest sense of the term, all religions are grounded in myths: beliefs about the world and nature that are transempirical. But a given religion's myth is not seen by members of that religion as simply one option among many; instead, it is understood to depict true reality. No doubt each myth acquires many accretions that, to the systematic theologian, may seem more cultural than creedal. But the point as it relates to the inclusivity/ exclusivity paradox is that the average member of religious organizations makes no such distinction.

To assert that all members of a congregation claim substantive reality for their rituals is likely an overstatement, but I am convinced that almost all worshipers feel that there is a true reality behind their worship and their creeds. They may well recognize that their rituals are human creations, but at the same time they are convinced that those rituals accurately reflect the "really real." They may acknowledge that they do not know the whole truth, but they will assert that what they do know is true. Like Paul, they know that they see "through a glass darkly" and that they may someday see "face to face" (1 Cor. 13:12), but they also believe that what they see here and now will turn out to be absolutely true about God and about life.

It is easy for religious leaders to forget that although they have studied religion in general, their congregations embrace a religion in particular. Parishioners do not usually make the distinction made by Immanuel Kant when he asserted that he had given up "believing" in order that he might "have faith." Their religious convictions are but extensions of their daily problem solving, in which the reality of the outside world is assumed by virtue of the operation of the five senses. The wooden table is real; God is real. Both exist, ultimately in the same manner. Faith that gives meaning to life and is grounded on that which goes beyond the five senses and cannot be proven by them, such as Kant affirmed, requires more subtle thinking than the average religious person is capable of.

Consequently, many church members interpret inclusive ideas and ideals as threats. They feel that the content of the faith must be preserved at all costs against the dangers of the modern world. Thus, religious leaders who push the limits of exclusive beliefs are likely to meet anxious rejection, because religious convictions are thought to be more like the proofs of science than the speculative explorations of art.

Living with the Inclusivity/Exclusivity Paradox

How can religious leaders live with their own convictions about inclusivity while at the same time honoring their followers' need for exclusivity? As with other paradoxes discussed in this book, the initial step is to admit that the paradox exists. To deny that in every religious organization—conservative and liberal alike—there are nonnegotiable principles that people hold dear would be to put one's head in the sand, like the proverbial ostrich. It is crucial for leaders to recognize the important role these principles play in social and personal identity. This recognition should lead to sensitive caution about challenging those principles by a too-facile inclusivity that group members might consider anathema.

Open acknowledgment that adherence to certain beliefs differentiating one's group from others is a social reality can lead, in the second place, to an explicit attempt to identify and state those convictions. Leaders should engage members of the organization in a discussion of the religious convictions that are unique and that provide the group with its social identity. It may sound like a pedantic exercise to group members when the leader first asks, "What are the convictions that make us different?" but after the leader explains that it is important for groups to openly state these convictions from time to time, the process seems more reasonable. Members may initially be suspicious of leaders who don't seem to know these beliefs already, but an open discussion of these matters solidifies the group as well as identifies areas where leaders should be cautious.

The importance of being explicit about group distinctiveness was acknowledged in a recommendation given to Fuller Theological Seminary by the executive secretary of the American Association of Theological Schools (AATS) in the early 1980s. Since its inception in the 1950s, Fuller had moved steadily away from a separatist stance toward a more conciliatory, cooperative posture with regard to other theological schools. The AATS executive secretary had been invited to address the seminary board of trustees on the future of theological education in the United States. He surprised the trustees with what he had to say. "I would stop trying to be so collaborative," he suggested. "I would return to my roots and emphasize Fuller's distinctiveness in the years ahead. It is the only way I think you will survive." What the AATS secretary knew was what Dean Kelley concluded about local churches: differentness sells, while similarity confuses. When students are deciding where to go to seminary, they choose a seminary that is distinctive. If all seminaries are alike, they are likely to go to the one nearest their homes. "Fuller will not survive by becoming like every other seminary in America" was the AATS secretary's observation.

The third step is to be intentional in one's leadership. As a routine approach, this means that religious leaders should identify "downward" rather than "upward." When contemplating some move toward inclusivity they should ask themselves, "How will this action be experienced by the average member of my church?"

Though there may be times when inclusivity becomes a moral obligation, as it was for the Southern ministers who met to discuss racial issues, these times should be limited in light of the sociological fact that group cohesion is strongly based on individual identification with the distinctiveness of the group. With this in mind, religious leaders would do well to be very cautious about any action that would threaten the group's distinctiveness.

At one level this may seem to be a recommendation that religious leaders prostitute themselves to the opinions of their followers; it is not meant to be so. I think it can be assumed that leaders of given groups would not hold those positions if they themselves did not agree with the essential convictions of the group to begin with. Remaining committed to those basic convictions should, therefore, not be as troublesome as it might seem. When I recommend identifying downward rather than upward, I am thinking of how easy it is, nevertheless, to succumb to the temptation to seek the approval of those above us—be they denominational or community leaders—instead of those beneath us. Filtering opportunities to become inclusive through the "average-member sieve" may seem bothersome at times, but it is a surefire way to maintain a group. As John F. Kennedy asserted in his book *Profiles in Courage*, leaders have to be politicians before they can be statesmen—that is, leaders have to have constituencies that elect them before they get the chance to vote their convictions in Congress. It would be a foolish bargain for leaders to act inclusively and then realize they didn't have a group to back them up.

On the other hand, acting with caution in inclusive ways doesn't mean ruling out inclusivity altogether. The discreet approach required was illustrated by a United Methodist minister in the southeastern United States who played golf each Wednesday with a minister of a nearby Church of Christ. Neither minister advertised their golf playing to their church members. They simply left early in the morning and played at a course some distance from their homes.

The Church of Christ was a separatist church that believed in baptism by immersion only and worship services without musical instruments; it would not recognize the salvation of Methodists and believed that organ accompaniment in Methodist worship was not biblical. These firm convictions were considered by most Church of Christ members as nonnegotiable. The Methodists, in turn, felt that the Church of Christ was the worst example of fundamentalism. Their members insisted they were above all those exclusivistic beliefs. They, too, were unwilling to associate with the Church of Christ members. They would have been very suspicious to know that their pastor played golf with the pastor of such a church.

Beneath the rhetoric of each church, though, these ministers knew they shared many community interests and religious convictions in common. They were aware of church history and knew that these differences were variations on a theme, and certainly not worth dying over! Nevertheless, these two ministers recognized the attitudes of their parishioners and made a conscious decision not to cause offense. They intuitively knew that a good portion of the loyalty they enjoyed was due to underlying beliefs that one group was right and the other was wrong. They might not engage in outright attacks on the other group; nevertheless they chose not to confuse the situation by being seen together.

A fourth step is a sequel to the third step of embracing intentional leadership. Before compromising essential convictions, religious leaders should consult with church members. The members can be expected to be cautious, but research has shown that when people are consulted and a rationale is explained, there is a significant tendency for them to support leaders' decisions. Accompanying the sociological fact that group identity is based on differentness is the psychological fact that people like to be consulted. Most people want to be wanted more than they want to be right. When people feel their opinions count and that they have had a chance to express them, they tend to trust leaders in launching out into unfamiliar territory.

Thus there are four steps involved in living with the exclusive/inclusive paradox: first, admit the paradox exists. Groups are built on exclusive beliefs, but they also share basic convictions with other groups. Second, lead group members in identifying which of their beliefs are nonnegotiable. Third, always be sensitive to how people react to attempts to be inclusive. And, fourth, intentionally consult leaders of the group before venturing out into inclusive territory.

5

Timely and Timeless

*Applying the Bible's Eternal Truths
to Present Circumstances*

Religious leaders can be more or less willing to be inclusive in their approach, as the previous chapter has shown. Similarly, they can choose a more or less conservative perspective on the issue of how to apply biblical teachings to present times.

The timely/timeless paradox refers to the tension that exists between recalling the timeless truths of the religious tradition and applying those truths in a timely fashion to current situations. There is much latitude for deciding how heavily to rely on the literal words of the Bible as opposed to current interpretations. That religious people can arrive at drastically different positions depending on how much weight they assign to one or the other side of this paradox can be seen in the current debates within the religious community on abortion and homosexuality.

Conservative Christian leaders have joined Roman Catholics in condemning abortion on the basis of the sacredness of life and the biblical proscriptions against murder. More liberal religious leaders, however, have taken the position that when the long-standing tradition of love, also biblically based, is applied to violations of women in rape and incest, abortion is an action that even Christ would approve of. Although both positions can be traced to ancient foundations, one point of view assigns higher priority to the timeless and explicit teachings of Scripture, while the other emphasizes a more liberal application of biblical principles to a modern situation.

A similar debate rages over whether homosexuality should be labeled a sin or be an acceptable (though alternative) lifestyle. In this case, scientific evidence unknown to people living just fifty years ago—far less to biblical writers—has concluded that there is a significant biological basis to homosexuality. Some religious leaders point to those places where the Bible seems to explicitly proscribe homosexuality, suggesting that just because a condition is biological, this doesn't of necessity excuse the resulting behavior. They note that heterosexuality is also biological but not all heterosexual behavior is condoned by religion. Others interpret these same Scriptures as disapproving only of promiscuity or debauchery, not committed and faithful relationships. They suggest that Jonathan and David were lovers, and the Bible would not have said so much about that relationship if it were not acceptable. Many in secular society would take as absolute truth the latest conclusions of the medical community on this issue, but religious leaders on both sides of this question would have difficulty with simplistic reasoning because they must also factor in biblical wisdom on the subject.

Jurists face a similar paradox in deciding how literally to interpret the Constitution of the United States in light of present-day realities. Some time ago, an article in *Newsweek* titled "Intent of the Framers" recounted a debate between then-Supreme Court justice William Brennan and U.S. Attorney General Edwin Meese over how the courts should interpret the Constitution. Meese took a stand parallel to that of religious leaders who tend to emphasize the role of Scripture and downplay the role of current experience in making decisions. He stated that modern courts should be limited by the original motives of those who wrote the Constitution. He was more conservative than Justice Brennan and more committed to what he felt was the inspired thinking of the framers of the Constitution.

Brennan, on the other hand, exemplified those religious leaders who want to emphasize the importance of current experience and downplay the role of Scripture in making decisions. He advocated taking seriously the passage of time between the writing of the Constitution and the late twentieth century, asserting that the framers of the Constitution did not live in modern society with its public schools, gang warfare, television, computers, and credit cards. He concluded it was arrogant to think that late-twentieth-century thinkers could accurately gauge what the writers of the Constitution might have intended for issues faced in the modern world. Moreover, he contended that while the principles of the Constitution are important, citizens in the modern age are at an advantage in having thought about those ideas for more than two hundred years and thus are able to apply their ideas creatively to current events.

Both Meese and Brennan were right, and both were wrong. It is not a case of either/or but of both/and, as most religious leaders come to realize. Although constitutional interpretation is, to some extent, an esoteric exercise practiced primarily in the halls of the Supreme Court (and only rarely in lower courts, where case law dominates), the debate over the meaning of sacred writings is daily fare for religious leaders. In fact, if I were to suggest the primary duty of religious leaders that distinguishes them from secular leaders, it would have to be the mandate to relate the past to the present. In business the past is forgotten, while in religion it is treasured. One of the root meanings of *religion* is "that which ties the eternal to the transitory, which binds the past to the present." Although both religious and nonreligious leaders might study the founding documents of their organizations, only religious leaders regularly relate truths written thousands of years ago to everyday life.

Exegesis and Exposition

Seminary professors teach future ministers that preaching should always include two facets: *exegesis* (the study of what the Scriptures meant to the writers themselves) and *exposition* (the proclamation of what these truths might mean for people living today). Both are essential to the foundational task of relating the timeless to the timely, that which Tillich called the Protestant principle in religion. He contended that the Protestant Reformation established for all time the necessity of reformulating the meaning of faith in contemporary terms. He was convinced of two things: that history would never outgrow its need for religion (life in every century asks questions to which faith is the answer) and that the answers of faith would always come from outside the situation (there is always a need for revealed truth that has stood the test of time).

Exegesis and exposition are necessary because much has happened since the beginning of most contemporary religious traditions. Further, many situations faced by modern people were never envisioned by writers of the Bible. It's a different world from that perceived by such comparative "moderns" as Emerson, Henry VIII, and Galileo, and that experienced by Saint Augustine, Aristotle, and the writers of the Old and New Testaments. With the rate of change accelerating rapidly, we will probably experience more changes in our lifetimes than did members of any previous generation. My father died in 1937, having never ridden in an airplane or viewed a sitcom on TV. My mother died in 1969 only days before an astronaut landed on the moon. Both would have been astounded by the idea of satellites orbiting the earth or people circling the earth in space stations. When photography was invented, it was immediately directed at a U.S. president, Abraham Lincoln, in stovepipe hat standing on a Civil War battlefield. No one could have imagined then that eventually a handheld camera would be able to instantly project images on a screen and insert them into a printed broadside.

Many moderns are so taken with scientific advances and technological progress, so sure that science and technology can meet all their needs, that they assume the Bible has no relevance anymore. These people would agree with the French astronomer and mathematician Pierre Simon de Laplace, who responded when Napoleon asked him early in the nineteenth century about the place of God in his theory of planetary motion: "Sir, I have no need of that hypothesis." Still, the Holy Bible will be read in all Jewish synagogues and Christian churches next Saturday or Sunday. Rabbis and ministers will take as their prime task interpreting these Scriptures and applying them to late-twentieth-century life. As one homiletics professor asserted, "Every sermon should begin or end in the heavenly Jerusalem—the Bible."

Like a number of Christians in the past, David Koresh was convinced that certain books of the Bible contained keys to historical events in the present and future. A few years ago, this nontraditional Christian teacher gathered a group of followers together in a compound outside Waco, Texas. The Seventh Day Adventist church, of which he had previously been a part, had disowned him for his radical view that Jesus' return was imminent. (Formerly they themselves had held this view as a central tenet—hence the term *adventist*—but history and a desire to be accepted in the larger society had tempered their expectations.) But what made Koresh so controversial was not his conviction that Jesus would return; even the most traditional and societally acceptable churches repeat the statement "Christ has died, Christ has risen, Christ will come again" in their Communion rituals. Most Christians look for the return of the Messiah, in a general sense. Although the Seventh Day Adventists and others explicitly distanced themselves from Koresh, he was simply reiterating in an objective manner the historic Christian faith. What got him into trouble was his style of communal living, his trading in guns, and his claim to being messianic himself—traits that crossed the line of acceptability. His refusal to surrender to authorities led to a fiery catastrophe in which he and many of his followers died.

Supposedly, Koresh's delay in responding to official demands was because he was busy studying the Bible. He was attempting to interpret the seven seals referred to in the Book of Revelations, hoping that he could find direction for himself and his followers. In this task, Koresh was doing what religious leaders have always done:

exegesis of the Scriptures to determine their meaning at the time they were written and exposition to determine what the implications of those teachings might be for the present. He was seeking to relate the timeless to the timely. The long delay in completing the task simply shows how difficult it can be. Those who stormed the compound seemed unable to respect or tolerate the need for time to complete the task. Regardless of what religious leaders might otherwise think of the Waco affair, most of them would comprehend Koresh's undertaking the role of asking the timely question of the timeless Scripture.

A less troubling outcome to asking the timely question of Scripture can be seen in a sermon preached at Christmastime by the minister of a suburban church in Southern California. She announced her sermon topic would be "Mary's pregnant! How about you?" When some members of the congregation read this sermon title in the weekly newsletter, they got on the phones and starting gossiping. "Have you ever heard of such a topic?" one said. "It sounds sacrilegious to me," proclaimed another. "I think this is one sermon I can miss," yet a third member was heard to say. "Oh, come on, give the minister a chance. It may be good, you never know," someone replied.

After the sermon on Sunday, many church members were glad they had come. They thought the minister had done an outstanding job of exposition, reflecting on an ancient event in an effort to apply its lessons to modern religious life. The minister described how the first chapters of the Gospel of Luke proclaimed that Mary was pregnant. Then she defined *pregnant* as "expectant," "full of promise and anticipation," "blossoming," "overflowing." She suggested that just as Mary bore the Christ child, those who followed Jesus should be full of his love toward other people. They should be pregnant, full of joy, eager to share their faith. The criticism died down. The task of witnessing to one's faith was accepted. The pastor did not deny the timeless truth of the Immaculate Conception; she creatively tied it to the timely truth of the need to share the faith.

The Methodist Quadrilateral Approach to the Timely/Timeless Paradox

The United Methodist church has attempted to address the timely/timeless paradox by delineating a "quadrilateral" model for exegesis and exposition. This model suggests that resolving the tension between eternal truths and current situations should be based on four interlocking considerations: the Bible and Holy Scriptures, religious tradition, human reasoning, and personal experience. In the past, this approach has used the analogy of a table with three legs to represent the relationships between these sources of authority. The Bible was conceived of as the tabletop (the beginning and prime authority for making religious decisions) and tradition, reason, and experience were seen as the three legs (the means by which the Bible is to be interpreted and applied).

Tradition refers to the way the church has interpreted the teachings of Scripture throughout its history. Tradition should be examined to see the degree to which there is consensus on interpreting and applying the Scriptures to a given contemporary problem. Reason, which includes both the findings of current natural science and those theological concepts that have current validity, is the attempt to logically relate current human understanding to the teachings of the Bible. Experience considers human relationships and individual histories.

For example, those churches that now ordain women as ministers relied on the quadrilateral process to decide upon this break from tradition. First, they surveyed the Bible for teachings on gender and ministry. The writings of Paul do seem to relegate women to a subordinate place in religious life. In 1 Corinthians 11:2 and following, he implies that man is to have authority over woman, that women are to veil their heads when they worship, and that man is "the image and reflection of God." According to 1 Timothy 3:1 and following, a bishop must be a married man who "must manage his own household." However, there are other Scriptures that make no such distinction. In fact, in the very chapter where Paul asserts woman's subordination he affirms equality by stating, "Nevertheless, in the Lord woman is not independent of man or man independent of woman. For just as woman came from man so man comes through woman; but all things come from God" (1 Cor. 11:11–12). More important, although all the disciples were men, Jesus made no distinction, and in fact many of his followers were women. Perhaps the strongest statement for equality came from Paul himself in Galatians 3:28: "There is no longer Jew or Greek, there is no longer slave or free, there is no longer male or female; for all are one in Christ Jesus."

After weighing the teachings of Scripture, these churches determined that although there is support both for including women in and for excluding women from the ministry, the bias is toward inclusion. Next, the theologians began to think about the issue, using reason to consider God's will in the present situation. They were unconvinced that tradition should have full sway, even though in Protestant and Catholic history only men seem to have been ministers. There were a few historians who asserted that the early church had had women ministers, although this practice didn't seem to last. The theologians decided that it was the will of God that every human being should consider what role to play in life, and ministry was just like any other role that might be considered. If a woman felt called into ministry and the church confirmed her, she should be ordained.

At this point, experience came into the picture. Even though few congregations had experienced having women ministers, most congregations had long had experience with women in ministry. In fact, the services and ministries of most congregations had primarily been led by women. Extending this experience to the pulpit and the sacraments seemed to require no great leap of faith. Thus, for more than a quarter of a century, many religious groups in the United States have welcomed women into the ordained ministry as a result of the quadrilateral process of decision making.

This quadrilateral model has been widely adopted by other Christian churches. However, the model doesn't definitively resolve the question of how to apply timeless teachings to timely concerns, because the interpretations suggested by tradition, reason, and experience are sometimes contradictory, as they are in the case of women's ordination. Even using this model, exegesis of the same Scriptures can differ from scholar to scholar. Nor does this model consider the fact that in exposition antagonists can use different Scriptures to prove their points. For instance, there are two creation stories in Genesis, each of which could bolster a different viewpoint. Genesis 2:21–22, "And the rib that the Lord God had taken from the man he made into a woman and brought her to the man," could be cited by those who insist that man is to hold authority in the church. Genesis 1:27, "So God created humankind in his image, in the image of God he created them; male and female he created them," could be relied upon by those who favor women's ordination.

Some religious leaders have suggested that these four sources of authority should be reconceived as resembling the *four* legs of a table. Those who take this position have concluded that the Bible is best understood as an ancient document written for a given time and place, with only general application to the issues of the late twentieth century. It is best for human beings to take the Bible seriously but not literally. From this point of view, the teachings of the Bible should not be taken as mandates but as general principles to be reflected upon in light of present experience, reason, and changing traditions.

As might be expected, this approach does not satisfy all religious leaders. Those who resist placing the Bible, reason, tradition, and experience on the same level feel that to change Scripture from a preeminent to a parallel place of authority is a radical departure from what Christians have done since the Bible was canonized more than a thousand years ago. At its extreme, this latter viewpoint contends that the Bible is divinely inspired and is to be considered inerrant and authoritative in all matters—both in the words it uses and the principles it recommends. In fact, some religious leaders state, "The Bible says it, I believe it, that settles it," while others contend that "Where the Bible speaks, we speak; where the Bible is silent, we are silent." This is almost equal to saying that there is no need for considering tradition, or reason, or experience. Historical criticism, used by almost all biblical scholars, has little or no meaning where such a position is taken.

Less extreme religious leaders affirm the primacy of the Bible in a different way. They do not look to the Bible as a book of science. In their exegesis, they accept the findings of biblical criticism yet feel that the writers of the books of the Bible were inspired, though human, as were the church fathers who selected those writings to be included in sacred Scripture. Thus, they still begin their inquiry into how to apply timeless truths to timely concerns by asking what Scripture says. They look for those special teachings that pertain to matters of faith and practice, or daily life. They seek to remain true to ancient wisdom while also being open to the way in which reason, experience, and tradition interpret, but do not confound, those teachings.

Living with the Timely/Timeless Paradox

As can be seen, the timely/timeless paradox is perennial and persistent in the life of religious leaders. There are always those in a given congregation who think that their religious leader should do more to preach from the Bible or apply ideas to daily problems. This inevitable dissatisfaction should be expected. Thus, as with other paradoxes we have considered, it is important to admit that this paradox is there and can never fully be resolved. Incorporating both the timely and the timeless in one's preaching and teaching is an ongoing task that must be faced and lived through. Admitting the complexity of the task is the issue. The approach that should be adopted is not to assume it can be done easily or finally.

Another approach to the timely/timeless paradox is to follow the admonition of Martin Luther to "love God and sin boldly." Recognizing the debatable outcome of almost all efforts to apply timeless truth to timely situations should not paralyze religious leaders. They should assert themselves with boldness, even if this is laced with a bit of humility.

As I've noted before, religious leaders have to speak far more frequently to their followers than do other leaders in our culture. On almost all of these occasions, they engage in exegesis and exposition. They should undertake this task with extreme self-consciousness and intentionality. As they prepare their presentations, religious leaders might well start by clearly deciding whether they will first attend to a problem currently being faced by their congregation or instead to a truth that arises out of the reading of Scripture. This is tantamount to asking "Shall I begin with the daily newspaper or the Bible?" It is choosing between the push of a contemporary problem and the pull of a biblical teaching. Though we may be in the habit of always beginning with one or the other, the approach should never be routinely made but always chosen reflectively and intentionally.

Another principle to follow in living with the timely/timeless paradox is to always be honest. Try not to bend the problem to fit the tradition or the tradition to fit the problem. Where leaders do such bending, they should be honest about it before their congregations: "I believe this problem we are facing is extremely important, but I could find no scriptural teaching about it. Nevertheless, I feel God's will on this matter is. . . . " Such honesty, when coupled with a willingness to dialogue, listen, profit, and change, goes a long way toward maintaining trust and cohesion in a congregation. In his delightful book *Consulting the Faithful*, Richard Mouw describes the value of talking with congregation members about religious issues. He suggests that far from being ignorant or misinformed on important issues, members can often teach religious leaders a thing or two.

It's critical for religious leaders to realize that most religious people still look to the Bible as a source of authority, holding it in mystical and reverential awe even if they haven't studied it. In a puzzling way, they want to know what the Bible states even though they think they already know. They don't realize that serious scholars find no uniform theology within its covers. They want to dialogue about exegesis and exposition. If the door for interaction is left open by religious leaders, there is a strong likelihood that congregational members will enter into discussion of the timely/timeless paradox with enthusiasm rather than with harsh judgment that emphasizes one option or the other.

Many who are familiar with the literary criticism that has contextualized the Bible within its own time and place still insist on biblical authority. Like Barth, they are still willing to claim that the Bible is still the "Word of God," in spite of its contradictions. Actually, the Swiss theologian felt that it is better to say that the Bible is a "testimony" to the Word of God and that in the Bible we have "the Word of God within the Word of God." Jesus Christ, for Barth, is the Word of God. The Bible is but a witness to that incarnate, or embodied, Word.

Barth has a suggestion for apprehending the timeless truths of Scripture that makes good theological sense even if its application might be a bit cumbersome. According to Barth, reading the Bible should begin with the four Gospels of Matthew, Mark, Luke, and John. After these, the Bible can be read backward to Genesis and then forward to Revelation. This process implies that one should look at the Bible's content through the lens of Jesus' life, death, and resurrection.

Barth carried his recommendations one step farther. He recognized that formalizing the sequence in which the Bible should be read does not readily resolve the disparity in the writing or answer the questions that arise week by week. As a practical approach, Barth suggested that the scriptures should be at the center of every worship service. Since, for Barth, the main task of the Bible is to proclaim the revelation of God in Jesus Christ, he proposed that Christian worship should be directed toward a reexperiencing of the risen Christ. Pastors are to read publicly a portion of the Bible from one of the four Gospels. Then they are to sit down, literally, and wait for the Holy Spirit to "bless the Word to the hearts of believers."

This idea of the Word of God being blessed to the hearts of believers implies that the timely/timeless paradox cannot automatically or easily be resolved. In fact, this recommendation for worship relies on a mysterious, miraculous process to make the transition from the past of Scripture to the present of a given time. It suggests that the only way that the timeless truth of God, revealed in Christ and testified to in the Bible, can be applied to the timely present is by a process of patient waiting for God. It is God, according to Barth, who resolves the paradox—not human beings weighing factors such as tradition, experience, and reason through their own mental processes.

Interestingly enough, God cannot be depended on to resolve the paradox on any predictable time schedule. All Barth contended was that it is possible that God will come from time to time and "bless the Word to the hearts of believers." At these moments, the believers become "contemporaries of Christ Jesus," from Barth's point of view. This means that they are able to think about contemporary situations with the mind of Christ. It is as if Jesus is present and is thinking through them about how to apply eternal truths to present events.

I find Barth's model for handling the timely/timeless paradox intriguing and theologically provocative. He wants to protect the power and initiative of God to influence human life; he doesn't trust human power by itself to accomplish this task. I'm not as pessimistic as Barth about human beings—particularly those leaders who faithfully and conscientiously approach the task—nor am I as willing as Barth to wait patiently for God to come on God's own time schedule. Nevertheless, I do honor the need that Barth emphasized for leaders to face the difficulties involved and to remain humble about their own insights in light of this most persistent and troublesome paradox.

Whereas these last two paradoxes have dealt with leadership approaches, there are other paradoxes that deal with the structure of religious organizations. We turn, now, to these.

Part III

. . . .

Paradoxes Built into the *Structure* of Religious Congregations

6

For-Profit and Not-for-Profit

*Balancing the Books While
Serving a Larger Purpose*

Religious organizations don't exist to make money; nevertheless, they must balance their financial books and pay their bills or they won't survive. This sad truth was illustrated by the circumstances of the closure of McCoy Memorial United Methodist Church in Birmingham, Alabama. Located across the street from the multiacre campus of Methodist-affiliated Birmingham-Southern College, McCoy Church served for almost a hundred years as the campus church. Many college ritual and festive events were held in its sanctuary. As time passed, the neighborhood surrounding the church and college changed to an almost totally black community. Many of the church's members moved away. When the denomination determined that it could no longer afford to keep up the buildings, it offered them for sale to anyone who would buy them, but to no avail—no buyers came. Finally, the United Methodists simply closed the doors of the church and walked away. There it sits today, on the edge of a thriving small college, a monument to yesterday's glory.

Although the purpose of the church was service, the reason for its closure was lack of profitability. Few religious leaders assert that they are out to make a profit, yet how many religious institutions would survive if they didn't have an excess of income over outgo at the end of the year? The task for leaders, then, is to lead in such a way that congregations don't neglect the truth that they must show a profit, while at the same time realizing that they don't exist for this reason.

It's important to note that although church income must be larger than expenses, these organizations can't be characterized as *profit making*, because they're not in business solely to turn a profit. Neither can we characterize these organizations as *nonprofit*. The only churches that can afford to be truly nonprofit—that is, not concerned about whether they make any money at all—are those that are supported or subsidized by the state, as in England. It's more often true that churches are *not for profit*, that is, their main aim is something other than making money even though making money is a necessity.

The Lutheran church in Sweden illustrates these concepts. The Swedish church will soon lose all state support, and the church tax that has filled its coffers in the past will no longer be available. It won't suddenly become a profit-making enterprise, but it will have to be much more attentive to its finances. It may heretofore have been nonprofit, in that it didn't have to worry about income and outgo, but I predict it will become explicitly not-*for*-profit in its outlook.

The tension between service and profit has generated debates in every century. The novel *Chameleon* by William X. Kienzle illustrates this paradox in modern society. Much of the plot centers around the debate in the Roman Catholic Diocesan Council of Detroit about whether to keep parochial schools open. The treasurer keeps reminding the council of the negative cash flow that the schools—even those in richer parishes—have incurred, and he recommends that the church shut down the schools. The education director, on the other hand, has given his life to parochial education and argues for keeping the schools open, stating that it's the duty of the church to serve the poor. The director of social services is a nun who lives in a changing neighborhood and knows the value of church education in enabling children to break out of the slums. She argues for shifting other monies to the schools. The diocesan legal advisor expresses fear that the church might be sued over an injury resulting from poorly maintained buildings. The bishop is caught in the middle, between warring factions not only on his council but also in his own heart, as he debates the costs of running a school system whose parents can no longer pay enough to keep it going.

The trustees of most private schools would close the doors immediately if a school didn't meet its expenses, much less show a profit, at the end of the year. Religious schools are different. Although service is their mission, the churches that sponsor them don't expect to make a profit. Still, the money needed to run the schools must come from somewhere, and thus religious leaders must concern themselves with raising funds even as they seek to serve a larger purpose.

The Need to Show a Profit

Saint Augustine noted in his treatise on the church, *The City of God,* that the church exists partly in heaven and partly on earth. As long as the church exists on earth, it has to engage in economic or commercial interaction with the environment. This rule applies to all religious activities, be they under the umbrella of a church or a parachurch organization, whether they take place under the auspices of the New Revelation Baptist Church in Compton, California; or the Trinity Broadcasting Company in New York City; or the faith mission ABECAR in Mogi das Cruzes, Brazil.

As the old saying goes, "Even gods must eat!" This is definitely true if the gods intend to exist for any length of time on earth. Unless the gods have resources we don't know of (and Jesus' cursing of the fig tree that had no figs on it in Matthew 21:18 implies they do not) they, and the organizations that bear their names, somehow have to buy or grow food if they intend to survive. Further, unless the gods choose to be modern hunter-gatherers, they have to have money, and unlike figs money doesn't grow on trees!

Engaging in some sort of profit-making transaction with the world is necessary for the gods and their successors who lead, and participate in, religious organizations.

The profit-making transaction can be as simple as collecting money from a few people who want to keep a church open. This is the case at Walker Memorial Church in rural Blount County, Virginia. Three generations of the Walker family are buried in the graveyard nestled against this white clapboard, one-room church on a dirt road some ten miles outside the nearest town. Even though almost all of the present-day Walkers have moved away from this area and the district is sparsely populated, worship services are still held at Walker Memorial twice monthly, and the church building is in an excellent state of repair. Why? Because the extended Walker family supplements the offerings of the few people who regularly worship at the church. Many Walkers return to the church for an annual homecoming each spring. They spend the whole weekend sharing memories, refurbishing the church, and cleaning the cemetery.

The profit-making transaction can also involve a commercial enterprise owned by a religious organization. There are many examples of such enterprises. One is a hotel in Oslo, Norway, owned by the Lutheran church. The church expects the hotel to turn over its profit for the church's mission endeavors. The manager of the hotel cannot make independent decisions about new services or major expenditures designed to increase business. He has to have approval for every endeavor other than setting standard hotel fare. Although the manager is a loyal churchman, I suspect that he is less motivated by the mission projects the hotel supports than by a desire to see the occupancy rate of his hotel stay high enough for him to report an excess of income over expenses at the end of the year. Moreover, the officials who hired him might have been concerned that he be a Christian supporting their mission projects, but it is likely they were much more interested in his record of experience in running hotels profitably.

Other commercial enterprises owned by religious organizations include Tony Alamo Fashions and the *Washington Times* newspaper. Some enterprises of this sort have a more explicitly religious reason for existence, but they are still concerned with making a profit. World Vision, for example, sends help to countries experiencing disaster. Still, no one expects them to go into debt to do it, or discounts their TV advertisements asking for financial help. Abingdon Press publishes religious material, but no one criticizes the business for taking out of print a book that isn't selling.

Once in a while, a religious organization's involvement in making business profits exposes the organization to scrutiny by the Internal Revenue Service. Where profit becomes the major motive, questions about the religious nature of the organization are asked. This is what got Sun Myung Moon in trouble with the IRS. Moonie theology contends that Jesus was sent by God to be the physical, as well as the spiritual, Messiah but that he failed to fulfill the physical part because he was crucified. Since it was God's intent that the Messiah accomplish this goal, he sent a new Messiah whose task it was to slowly but surely become ruler of the physical world. This involved buying such businesses as fishing fleets, manufacturing companies, and newspapers. Thus, Moon claimed that the profits of these enterprises should be considered religious, not secular. Many religious persons and groups, including the National Council of Churches, supported Moon even though his claim seemed somewhat extreme and there were allegations of personal fraud. They did this because of their belief in the importance of the separation of church and state—and because many of them also had secular investments that earned them money. Unfortunately, the courts did not agree, and they imprisoned Moon for income tax evasion.

A religious organization's involvement in making and managing business profits can raise other issues as well. For instance, there is the issue of whether a church takes into account matters of social justice and corporate responsibility when it invests its funds. Whereas there was a serious effort to promote divestiture in South

Africa before the ending of apartheid, other investments are sometimes not scrutinized as closely as they could be.

Despite all its complications for churches, showing a profit is certainly preferable to the alternative. When churches fail to show a profit, religious leaders must make hardheaded business decisions. In England, the Anglicans have regularly decided to close churches. The word *redundant* can be seen written on boarded-up churches throughout England and Wales. What this generally means is that few, if any, people attended that church anymore and the monetary offerings given by the attendees were not great enough to support the salary of the priest. This is true even though Anglican parishes are part of the Church of England, a state church that enjoys a stipend from the government and has ample resources to supplement the budgets of local parishes, and even though a number of Anglican churches in Britain are served by what are called nonstipended priests, who have other jobs but are willing to serve unprofitable churches without remuneration. The Anglicans are not sloppy businesspeople. They make hard decisions in regard to economic realities.

Another example of the hard decisions that must sometimes be made can be seen in the closing of the Fuller Evangelistic Association (FEA) in 1996. The FEA began earlier in this century as an adult church school class taught by Charles Fuller in the Long Beach (California) First Presbyterian Church. The class was very popular and soon outgrew the church. It moved to the city's convention center and began radio broadcasts on Sunday nights during the Second World War. The Old Fashioned Revival Hour, as the broadcast became known, was heard throughout the United States and attracted many servicemen listeners. The program outlasted both the war and the life of Charles Fuller, but support for the Sunday night services began to wane as television grew in popularity. After Fuller's death, a number of popular preachers were engaged to try to recoup the enthusiasm of the old model. None truly succeeded in spite of a name change and the establishment of a church consulting service. In the spring of 1996, the trustees decided to close the Fuller Evangelistic Association and sell the property. Paying the bills was the determining factor.

At the very least, then, any religious organization must break even financially or it has to close its doors. As noted earlier, Saint Augustine was fully aware of this truth about income and outgo. His book is replete with acknowledgments of the for-profit/not-for-profit paradox.

The Need to Serve a Larger Purpose

Churches raise money so that they can support endeavors that have nothing to do with making a profit. The real business of religion is service, without concern for recompense or reward. As mentioned earlier, parochial schools are one example of this motivation toward service; mission societies are another. Although fewer than 10 percent of the population of China have become Christians since missions began there over a century ago, churches still send missionaries. Churches don't expect to make a profit on their missions to China, either in terms of money or members. The Southern Baptist church's Christmas offerings for the Lottie Moon Mission raise many dollars for the work in China. No one expects a monetary profit from these gifts; rather, the giving is grounded in a conviction that these efforts result in changing human lives.

Silence, Shasako Endo's haunting account of Portuguese missions to Japan in the seventeenth century, illustrates this nonfinancial but human profit motive. The book proposes that yet another motive, faithfulness, can provoke religious behavior even under conditions of persecution. The principal character, a Catholic priest, persists in his mission even though the shoguns have undertaken a violent persecution designed to rid Japan of all traces of Christianity and the outside world considers Japan a "swamp" that will swallow up all nonindigenous religions such as Christianity. The Catholic priest in this story is typical of religious leaders everywhere.

They are in religious leadership to serve. They don't think of themselves as businessmen, but as servants.

This desire to serve no matter what the cost has been borne out
by studies of why persons go into ministry, as reported in *The Psychology of Clergy*, which I coauthored with Richard Hunt. There is
little question but that the prime motive of religious leaders is to
serve people and to share a religious way of life with them. In almost
every case, making money was last on the list of reasons. Most ministers work more than sixty hours a week, with only moderate financial support for their endeavors. None of the religious leaders I know
are "into" religion for profit. There are few if any Elmer Gantrys or
Jim Bakkers among them. It grates against their nerves to hear about
the profit-making side of this paradox. They simply don't think that
the organizations they lead are profit-making enterprises, because
they're not in religious work to make money.

It has always been of interest to me as a psychologist to realize
that most of the missionaries and theologians who teach with me
don't know what their next year's salary will be. Psychology professors always know; they bargain with the administration over raises
and perks. But these others, who are overt religious leaders by trade,
seem relatively unconcerned about the issue. They typically define
their roles in not-for-profit terms, and they tend to think of *profit* as
a dirty word.

I encountered a clear example of the not-for-profit point of view
when I consulted to the psychology department of Brigham Young
University some years ago. As we drove onto the campus, my host,
an eminent social scientist, said, "Did I tell you that I've become a
bishop?" I was astounded. Knowing that being a bishop was a full-
time, well-paid job in my church, I asked, "Oh, does that mean
you've given up being a psychologist?" "Oh, no," he replied, "I'll do
them both; being a bishop in my church is a voluntary job done in
one's spare time." Then he shared that being a Mormon bishop took
about twenty hours a week of volunteer time with not a penny in

recompense, even for expenses. Questions like "How much will you earn?" or "Will you be given a house to live in?" or "They'll at least cover your expenses, won't they?" were not my friend's concern. He had no interest in financial profit or personal gain.

Even the trustees of the foundation that undergirds the budget of Trinity Church on Wall Street in New York City would never picture themselves as overseers of a profit-making enterprise, in spite of the likely fact that their investments calculatedly show a return on capital exceeding that earned by most Fortune 500 companies. Further, leaders at Princeton University School of Theology, which boasts endowment resources exceeding $400 million, would speak demurely of their administrative goals in service terms and would never refer to last year's profits on investments as the main focus of their annual report.

These examples are typical. Religious organizations almost universally present themselves as offering service regardless of the recipient's ability to pay and apart from return on their investments of time and money. They simply do not understand their efforts in terms of income and outgo. In fact, they would tend to use the word *nonprofit* to describe themselves. My contention that no organization is nonprofit would be shrugged aside as an unimportant distinction.

Living with the For-Profit/Not-for-Profit Paradox

The crux of the for-profit/not-for-profit paradox is that neither motive can totally dominate the life of a religious organization; nor can it be ignored without resulting in failure. Both are focal issues that must be faced and held in tension if religious institutions are to thrive and not just survive. Often, the fact that religious leaders are motivated by service rather than money translates into a disinterest in or disdain for the business affairs of the religious organizations they lead. They leave those issues to others. However, for religious leaders to deal creatively with this paradox, they must acknowledge its essential religious importance and incorporate conscious attention to it into their professional self-understanding. Then they must encourage their lay leaders and members of the congregation to pay the same conscious attention to both sides of the paradox.

Most religious leaders find their parishioners more attuned to the need for profit than they are. For example, a young pastor bemoaned the action of her trustees in turning down the request of a youth program to use a church building. She claimed that the trustees had no vision, nor did they have enough compassion for the needs of youth in their community. But the trustees were aware that the gymnasium that she wanted to offer to the youth program had been out of debt for only eighteen months and that the weekly offerings by the members were only barely meeting the budget—a budget that included her salary. They were very cautious about the possible damage that could be done to the new building by nonchurch groups as well as the financial responsibility they might incur for accidents on their property. Like many trustees, they wanted to safeguard their resources. The pastor felt they were selfish, but they saw themselves as prudent.

Clergy as well as lay leaders need to keep both sides of the paradox in mind when they make decisions. Further, they need to bring this tension under the umbrella of a theological rationale. Religious groups are in business, but they are not businesses. They exist for a higher goal. They have a responsibility to use wisely that which has been entrusted to them, and this wisdom includes both willingness to risk in the service of ideals and restraint not to squander their resources. In the illustration above regarding the gymnasium, the pastor represents the willingness to risk and the trustees represent cautious restraint. Each needs to acknowledge the validity of the other's point of view.

The University Baptist Church in Fort Smith, Arkansas, illustrates the use of theological rationale in financial decisions. The church no longer takes up an offering in any worship service. Its leaders in charge of finance decided that they would adopt the practice of "seeker churches" that have intentionally designed their services to draw in nonchurch folk who are suspicious of religion's appeal for funds. They put offering plates at each of the doors and tell people that they can put their gifts into the plates when they leave the church. They explained to the congregation that they weren't going to talk money in church anymore but were going to trust each person to prayerfully consider how much God was calling him or her to give to the work of the church. They lifted up the parable of the talents and Jesus' observation of the "widow's mite" (Luke 21:2). This case shows that hard-nosed trustees, whose job it is to see that the church doesn't go into debt, can be convinced to follow a radical approach to financing so long as they understand the situation from a theological point of view.

In religious organizations, money matters should be well understood by members as well as leaders. Understanding of the nature of the church as a not-for-profit organization must be communicated again and again to the members of the congregation. When churches sell "Brunswick stew" to the community, as one church in Wisconsin does on a monthly basis, those who prepare the stew and deliver it should be well aware that the money that is collected is intended for service. Further, parishioners should realize that when they are asked to pay a rental fee for the use of the church hall for a private celebration of some kind, the fee will be used to extend the services of their congregation. Freedom from paying the rental fee is not a perquisite of membership, such as might be offered to members of the local country club.

Beyond the general concept that financial issues should be understood and dealt with at all levels of the religious organization, there is the question of how best to handle the economics of running a church. In the past, some have touted "zero-based budgeting" as the ideal method for churches. Following this model of budgeting, leaders agree to spend all their funds in the year in which the monies are raised—on either programs or gifts. They spend what is given and trust God to fill the well again when a new need arises. At times, the approach has been espoused with the theological justification that this is what it means to trust God completely to provide for future needs. Some modern seeker churches promote this sort of thinking and criticize churches that base their budgets on pledges, suggesting that this shows too little faith in God.

"Launching out on faith" has been the motto of many religious organizations, and one has to admit that it sometimes works. However, not treating the church or parachurch enough like a business also has its pitfalls. Very little in the form of major expenditures can be undertaken on the basis of one year's income. Lake Avenue Congregational Church in Pasadena, California, has been worshiping in a magnificent multimillion-dollar sanctuary for more than five years. The sanctuary would never have been built had the leaders used zero-based budgeting; the congregation will be paying on the mortgage for this new building for at least the next fifteen years. Undertaking this project provoked church leaders to apply every profit-making principle they could muster. Their projections of how much income would be necessary to service the construction loan were thoroughly considered. They recognized that even under the best of conditions there was a danger that the church would default. Some might say that such an undertaking took as much "launching out on faith" as any year-by-year trust in God does.

Most religions operate somewhere in between profit making and zero-based budgets. They do keep their eyes on future needs and at times lay aside monies for expected expenditures. If they do not, no new buildings will be built. Although they accept monies to undergird certain types of ministries or to provide for certain needs in perpetuity, they don't casually build up excesses just for the purpose of having large bank accounts. They are in the business of service, and they recognize that this is the motive behind the gifts that are entrusted to their care. This approach takes into consideration the paradox of knowing that the prime goal is service but that in the modern world it takes money to help people.

My hope is that, facing the fact that their organizations were not made in heaven but on the contrary are located here on earth, religious leaders will look at the for-profit/not-for-profit paradox as an opportunity to lead their members to tolerate the tension this paradox produces and work with it in creative planning. Whereas all organizations must do business with their environment through programs and products that generate income, religious organizations need not become secular businesses nor give up their high ideals. It is possible to be successful and faithful at the same time. Using money wisely may turn out to be the most religious thing that church groups can do.

7

Person and Organization

*Running an Efficient Organization in Which
People Feel Deeply Recognized*

The for-profit/not-for-profit paradox is built into the structure of the church itself, as the previous chapter made apparent. Another structural paradox, inherited the moment a new religious organization files its "fictitious name statement" in the newspaper, is the person/organization paradox. Regardless of whether the organization is Mission Aviation Fellowship or the Holy Name Lutheran Church, the truth that people have personal reactions to organizational decisions cannot be denied. Religious leaders must make decisions about programs, personnel, and property to keep the organization running, but they must also expect that not every member of the church will be pleased with every decision. If they assume that members are always supportive and understanding simply because they are religious people, they are bound to be disappointed.

A good example of this paradox occurred in one church in a dispute over the budget. The pastor asked leaders about a couple he had not seen at church recently. "They've quit coming," someone reported. "Why?" "They didn't like the way we handle finances; we ask people how much they will give and then determine the budget on the basis of these pledges. They thought we should determine the budget first and then ask people to pledge money to it." The pastor immediately expressed surprise that this would cause the couple to quit attending church. They did have the chance to state their opinion in the finance committee meeting, and people did listen but voted to retain the old pattern. So why did the couple have hard feelings, when the vote was fair and square?

On further reflection, the pastor remembered that this couple were fundraising professionals who were active in garnering major monetary support for another institution in the community. Thus their egos were apparently involved in the issue and in their decision to leave. Nobody enjoys feeling like a member of a minority, and nobody likes to be unable to persuade others, especially about a concern where one has some expertise.

This pastor, like so many others, failed to realize that church members have strong emotional reactions to decisions that are made, reactions that may have nothing to do with what is best for the organization. Furthermore, generally no member is pleased with everything an organization does, even though the member needs the organization because almost nothing would get accomplished without it. The paradox leaders face is that they must execute group plans and procedures while never forgetting that people experience organizational life individually and personally.

Religious leaders are susceptible to thinking that because love is the norm in the religious organization, members function on a higher plane than do members of secular organizations. Leaders may think that church members should share a family-type relationship in which everyone understands and accepts whatever the organization does without murmur or question. It just isn't so. Religious organizations are no different from other groups. Members complain; members argue; members resist. Members of religious organizations do not passively accept everything leaders decide should be done. In reality, dissension may be even more prevalent in religious organizations than others. All the talk about how they are a family whose members love each other flies out the window when religious groups do something that displeases members. The old saying that there is no fight like a church fight may be as true as today's sunrise.

Religious persons also have high expectations of how they'll be treated by religious leaders—expectations that leaders don't always live up to. A religious organization is a place where good feelings are touted but bad feelings are likely to arise. A surprising number of individuals report that even though at times they experience deep feelings of inspiration and exhilaration as members of religious groups, they have also experienced even deeper feelings of being misunderstood, mishandled, and misperceived.

Members who withdraw from religious groups often do so with strong feelings. On the one hand, they have a sense of personal guilt over their awareness that as religious persons they *should* be understanding, supportive, and forgiving of others in the group, but they no longer feel that way. On the other hand, they have a sense of angry blame about their expectation that leaders of religious groups should practice what they preach: though leaders should be compassionate and concerned about members' feelings, they often seem not to care. These disaffected members don't feel they are treated as they should be in an organization that espouses compassionate values.

Thus, with this paradox religious leaders walk a tightrope. They must realize that members react emotionally, and they act on those emotions because they are motivated by self-interest. They must also realize that love is the norm in religious organizations, which means the leaders are expected to show a level of compassion and sensitivity when planning programs and making decisions that is not required of secular leaders. Explicit attention to sharing and dialogue is essential if religious leaders are to hold both sides of this paradox in tension.

Religious Behavior Is Motivated by Self-Interest

Some thirty years ago, Harvard psychologist Gordon Allport designed a scale to measure intrinsic and extrinsic motives for religious behavior. He assumed that people participated in churches either because they were interested in religion for religion's sake (an intrinsic motive) or because of some extraneous reason not related to religion at all (an extrinsic motive). He presumed that intrinsically motivated people worshiped God out of love of God, not out of any personal good they could get out of it, while extrinsically motivated people went to church for the fun they had, the social contacts they could make, or the personal benefits religion brought to their lives. Much research using the I-E (intrinsic-extrinsic) measure has shown that there are probably few if any purely intrinsically motivated people. Most people are interested in some benefit that religion brings to them.

Jean-Jacques Rousseau formulated a similar idea more than two hundred years ago. In his theory of the "social contract" he proposed that people interact with one another in a kind of mutual exchange: they give of themselves in order to get something in return. He suggested that reciprocity is the prime reason people overcome self-interest and join together to accomplish any task. It is also the reason people obey rules and laws. Thus, were Rousseau alive today, he would claim that citizens drive their cars on the right in order not to be hit by the cars coming toward them—purely self-interested behavior.

Religious leaders who expect members to participate no matter what—and who are shocked when people complain or withdraw—are forgetting that people come to church because they expect to get something personal out of the experience. Religious behavior is purely voluntary: people *have to* work to make a living, but they don't have to go to church. Leaders seem easily to forget that the church members are not required to be there as they (the leaders) become habituated to their roles in religious groups. They would do well to remember that, as the management theorist Peter Drucker once stated, "Religion lives off the excess of culture; no one has to be religious." One minister clearly acknowledged recognizing this when he proclaimed at the start of each worship service, "Welcome!

I hope you find what you are looking for here today and that you will come again."

The fact that some people don't find what they're looking for—that they complain or withdraw—isn't always the fault of religious organizations that don't practice what they preach. It's possible that some reactions are firmly based in personal misperceptions of religious organizations, about which leaders know nothing. Many of the cases I use in my workshops on conflict management are of this type. Called "woodwork problems" because they're like termites that appear in the woodwork, these are the kinds of crisis that appear suddenly and over which leaders have no control. These problems demonstrate that getting complete control of the situation is impossible.

One new pastor had been at a church for less than six months when he faced a woodwork problem. He noticed that a certain family opposed every new program idea that was suggested by the church council. They even opposed having a Christmas pageant that had been a church tradition for years. Since this family was large enough to sabotage almost any program, he went to their patriarch and asked what the matter was. It turned out that twelve years earlier, their high-school-age daughter had fallen in love with the son of a family that happened still to be holding many of the top leadership positions in the church when the new pastor arrived. The son was a talented and attractive high school football player. He and the young woman had made plans to get married, but then he was recruited to play football by the state university. When he went off to college, he fell in love with someone else. He broke off the engagement, and it crushed the young woman. Her family had never forgiven him—or his family—for breaking their daughter's heart. Now they were resisting the pastor's plans because the initiatives came from members of the other family.

The new pastor was perceptive enough to sense the problem early in his ministry and to evoke enough confidence in the offended family that they would share their pain with him. This is a clear case of people reacting negatively to congregational plans for reasons of self-interest that had little or nothing to do with the church at large.

Love Is the Norm, But Not Always the Reality

The fact that religious behavior is motivated by self-interest doesn't preclude or contradict the expectation that religious organizations are places where unselfish love is expressed. 1 John 4:19 states: "We love because He first loved us." Ideally, for Christians, self-interest needs have been met by God's love of them seen in Christ. In theory, they no longer need to act selfishly because their need for love has been satisfied. Thus, they can now act to meet the self-interest needs of others by unselfishly loving them.

The chorus of a well-known hymn ends with the assertion that "They will know we are Christians by our love." In religious organizations, in contrast to secular ones, love is the norm. People expect more humaneness, understanding, sensitivity, unselfishness, and compassion from religious organizations—be they churches or religious businesses—than they do from nonreligious groups. But these expectations aren't always fulfilled. Almost everyone has had the experience, at one time or another, of feeling that the practice didn't exemplify the ideal.

Consider the after-service coffee hour. In one church I know, the associate minister welcomes people to worship and encourages them to attend the coffee hour after the service is over. He concludes by saying, "There will be many people there [at the coffee hour] who will surround you with interest and a warm welcome." But many first-time attenders who venture into after-service coffee hours report it is the loneliest hour of the week. In spite of what ministers state, strangers often remain strangers. Friends talk to friends, families greet families—but few members talk with newcomers. Others

report how difficult it is for them to break into the friendship pat-
terns of churches when they move into new communities.

It's interesting to compare the experience of first-time attenders
at local churches with that of people who walk into a Radio Shack
store in a shopping mall. Radio Shacks have electronic bells that
ring when a person enters the store. Customers are immediately
greeted by a clerk and asked if they need help in finding what they
want. (Interestingly, this is the same language the minister uses in
his welcome.) Yet in traditional churches very few members come
up and welcome strangers with as much intention as Radio Shack
clerks do. I would guess that almost no newcomers to meetings of
religious organizations are directly asked, "Can I help you find what
you're looking for?" Out of respect for privacy, or at worst disinterest, many religious organizations fail to inquire into the personal
interests of strangers.

These same religious organizations may be quick to level the
criticism against *new* religions that they manipulate people's need
for friendship. What this usually means is that these groups intentionally act friendly and solicitous to newcomers. For example, they
often assign members to be companions of those who are new to the
group. The Moonies, for example, specifically recommended that
their members "love-bomb" potential converts with affection, interest, and companionship. They frequently met buses coming into
such cities as San Francisco and identified youth who looked lost
and confused. Then they invited these young people to supper and
offered them a place to sleep. Invitations to weekend retreats and
weeklong camps followed. The newcomers were constantly exposed
to friendly companionship.

Is this type of attention to newcomers only "manipulation," as
some have charged? The accusation is that these groups don't really
mean their "love bombing"; they have some ulterior purpose in
mind, such as recruiting new members. It's hard to know the true
motives of those who start new religions, but if getting members is

their aim, this doesn't make them much different from traditional churches (whose evangelistic efforts are less successful). At least the Moonies practiced what they preached. One member reported that even after ten years in the group, he looked upon the first two months of membership as the happiest time in his life.

The Jonestown (Guyana) massacre in 1979 claimed the lives of two children of the pastor of the First United Methodist Church in Reno, Nevada. The following Sunday, the pastor said that although he mourned their loss, his children "received more acceptance and love in their year in People's Temple than they received in their whole life in the Methodist church." In response to such a statement about the warmth experienced by persons in nontraditional religious groups, perhaps all that other religious groups can say is "We don't do that." The question might be asked, "Why don't you? You talk about love, companionship, and friendship all the time. Why don't you practice it intentionally? It's only manipulation when you don't believe in it and do it as means to the wrong ends."

Turning from the absence of overt altruism and concern to a more serious matter, it's not uncommon for people to report that they have experienced no difference between the decision-making practices of religious organizations and those of secular organizations to which they belong. In nonreligious groups, it's sometimes true that little attention is paid to the impact of leaders' actions; further, many business decisions seem to be made out of a prime concern for reputation rather than for the concerns of people. Religious groups are expected to make decisions that put people first, but sometimes they do not. This has led some members to withdraw, claiming that they were not treated with love and consideration of their humanness.

A prime example of this occurred when the music committee of one church suddenly decided to terminate the contract of the adult choir director. A talented musician, she was deeply appreciated by the members of the choir and by many in the congregation. She had a good sense of ministry and participated in the worship services with skill and discernment. On special occasions, such as Mother's Day and Father's Day, she created choruses of almost a hundred participants. She was sincerely admired, and most members of the choir were looking forward to singing under her direction for many years to come. However, unknown to those who saw her only on Sundays, she was experiencing some disagreements with those who were involved in other parts of the music ministry of the church. Their differences reached a climax over decisions relating to a summer tour of the youth choir. Suddenly in late June, the music committee decided not to renew her one-year trial contract. Within a week she was gone.

The way the news was broken to the choir indicated a complete lack of sensitivity to their feelings. The church organist announced the change when members of the choir came for their last rehearsal in June. The flowers, music stands, peppermint candy, and pencils the director had always provided were no longer there. She and her "goodies" had just vanished!

Many members of the choir were bewildered by this sudden change. The chair of the music committee stopped by toward the end of the rehearsal and explained the firing this way: "If you have a person who works on an assembly line in your business who is underperforming, you tell them how to upgrade their skills. However, the music director is more like a vice president. If a vice president isn't in agreement with the thrust of your company, you relieve them of their duties. This was the case with the music director. She didn't see eye to eye with us on the way the program should go, so we didn't renew her contract."

Although the choir members pressed him for more details, the music director wouldn't answer their questions. He brushed aside the concerns of those who felt the decision was made too quickly and seemed insensitive to the angry and hurt emotions arising among those who had become devoted to her leadership. He acted as if they should accept the decision as would members of a corporation whose leaders had just issued a business decree.

Mutinous feelings swept through the choir. Many members felt that the comparison the music committee chair had made between a production worker and a vice president didn't exactly fit their situation at the church. They talked about the incident a lot among themselves. One member put it this way: "The committee didn't seem to take into consideration who we are. We are volunteers. We are also the church. How can they be so blind? We are not a company; we are the church. We should be nicer to each other than this. Don't they know they might wake up one Sunday and there would be no choir? We could boycott the service! I think we ought to tell them how we feel." This church was very fortunate that in fact the choir remained faithful; not a single member left. The way the decision was handled could have had serious repercussions. After all, the music committee didn't include the members of the choir in their decision, nor did they offer a full explanation of why the director was fired. No provisions were made for mourning or for honoring her year of good leadership.

In fairness, it should be said that not all *non*religious organizations ignore human feelings and treat people as pawns to be moved around without due consideration. An organization, religious or not, is a group of persons who fulfill their lives while meeting a human need. This definition combines mission and maintenance, production and personal needs. My brother-in-law, a chief executive officer for an Australian company, once said to me, "At the end of my career, if I feel I have assisted in the life-fulfillment of the eleven persons just beneath me, I will consider myself a success." "But aren't you interested in the bottom line—in making a profit?" I asked. "Of course I am," he replied. "But I know that if I play a part in fulfilling their lives, they will make money for me." In his perceptive book *Leadership Is an Art*, Max De Pree expresses agreement with this philosophy when he says, "To be a leader means, especially, having the opportunity to make a meaningful difference in the lives of those who permit leaders to lead."[1] He goes on to list eight basic rights of workers: to be needed, to be involved, to have a covenantal relationship, to understand, to affect one's own destiny, to be accountable, to appeal, and to make a commitment. A better statement of practical love would be hard to find.

Living with the Person/Organization Paradox

Even though the person/organization paradox can never be transcended, most leaders can minimize its effects if they're willing to try. Religious leaders should recognize that decisions must be made, and no decision pleases every member. Attention to the way organizational decisions are made and executed should be a leader's constant preoccupation. Every decision, even if reached by a consensus vote of church officers, should be followed by asking, "How will people feel about what we have done?" This means that as much thought should be focused on the reaction as on the decision. Although this approach extends the time of deliberation, it allows for the kind of forethought required to deal sensitively and compassionately with people's feelings.

To follow up this approach, as many decisions as possible should be interpreted to the members as being "tried for a time" rather than "written in stone." This can't be done for every decision, but it can become the norm more often than might be thought. During trial periods, reactions should be invited and heard. Where people feel they have a voice, they often support the very issue they once opposed. Then, too, officials can improve their decisions by considering the suggestions they receive.

Further, religious leaders should integrate pastoral work into their administration of the organization. It's well known that groups finding themselves voting in the minority or feeling marginalized retreat, surrender, or engage in mutiny. Leaders should follow up administrative decisions with visits to those who did not get their way. They should listen and affirm those perceived to have negative feelings about decisions that were made.

Finally, although religious leaders ultimately have responsibility for administration of their organizations, they should turn over as many decisions as possible to volunteer officials. They should remain program-neutral in the sense that they don't become overly involved in *how* something is accomplished (the program) but remain committed to *what* their group intends to do (the final goal). Goals and techniques should be kept separate so that in going to offer pastoral care to those who did not win the votes leaders evoke trust and identification. This is a difficult task but one that can be accomplished to a great degree if leaders try to do it.

Some time ago psychologist William Wallace studied the effect of sharing decisions in religious organizations. He found that church members who had a chance to talk with officers, hear the officers' rationale for the decisions, and share their own personal opinions were far less likely to withdraw from participation if decisions were made with which they disagreed. Although they were unable to change what church officers decided to do, they felt heard and understood. The result? They were far more likely to remain in the group. Often, they became supportive of the decision even when they didn't agree with it.

The difference that sharing decisions can make is illustrated by another case having to do with the firing of a church music direc-tor. In this case, the way the situation was handled showed that the leaders understood well the person/organization paradox. The prob-lem this church had with its choir director was known to the lead-ers but not widely among the parishioners. The director was well liked by the choir members but had problems with his personal finances. He had failed to pay back loans taken from the church and misused church funds without recompense. The church officials had warned him about these matters and confronted him with the poor example he was setting. When things went from bad to worse, the leaders decided to relieve him of his duties.

During the next worship service, the pastor announced the fir-ing and stated that ten members of the church board would be available after the service to explain more fully why the decision had been made. He then asked these leaders to stand so worshipers would recognize them and designated places around the church where they would be available. For almost an hour after the service, the leaders talked with those who sought them out. They expressed the pain and difficulty the church board had gone through in having to fire such a loved and skilled member of the staff. This process seemed to be well received, and the transition to a new choir director in this church seemed to be made with little resistance and opposition.

This kind of explicit attention to sharing and dialogue would be very rare in the business world. Having people available to explain a potentially controversial decision on a one-to-one basis showed that the church officers were sensitive to how personally members react to what goes on. These leaders didn't treat their religious organization as they might have treated an employer. They were sensitive to the paradox that exists in organizations that are voluntary yet advocate acceptance, support, and good relationships.

The relationship between persons and organizations is never perfect. To be part of an organization is to join with others in accomplishing tasks that no one person can accomplish alone. Such collaboration requires compromise; no one is ever fully pleased. As the mother superior of a convent once stated in a booklet of rules she wrote for her sisters, "I write these rules so that we may accomplish our goals without killing each other." The stress that people experience in religious organizational life is an inevitable product of the fact that membership is voluntary and motivated by self-interest, and that although they are touted, the ideals of love and friendship are seldom fully practiced. Knowing this is true can change the way religious leaders do business. They can pay attention to sharing decisions, show concern for those who disagree, and monitor their behavior so that any tendency they might have to run roughshod over other people is strongly resisted.

Note

1. De Pree, 1989, p. 11.

Part IV

. . . .

Paradoxes of Congregational Mission

8

Product and Process

Valuing Ends and Means Equally

In the religious enterprise, how something is done is as important as the end product. Within the context of the organization's mission to deepen faith, the paradox can be seen in the case of a group of leaders who met to plan a work-team experience for church youth. The youth counselors began meeting in early October to plan the experience, which was to construct a new dormitory for an orphanage in Tecate, Mexico, during the week before Easter the following spring.

Present at the first meeting to plan the experience were the four counselors (who were parents of two of the youths), the pastor, and the four officers of the high school group itself. The pastor pointed out that there was a twenty-year tradition of Easter work camps for the youth of the church, so many of the details had already been ironed out. If the minutes of past planning groups were followed, the task of planning for the camp should not be too difficult. This sounded good to the committee members since they were all busy people; they expected to attend the work camp but didn't want to spend too much time and energy planning the event. The first meeting ended with a round of prayers for guidance and an agreement to meet again in early November.

Monthly meetings went off with very little disagreement and the time for the Easter work camp arrived with all plans in place. As scheduled, on Saturday morning at the beginning of the Easter recess, the bus rolled up to the church promptly at 9:00 A.M. to pick up the counselors and thirty-two youths and to take them to Tecate. The days passed quickly. Despite sunburns suffered by almost everyone and a leg scratch that needed some first aid, all the team members arrived home late the next Friday night tired but full of good stories to tell of their experience. Like those who had gone before them on the Easter work teams, many of the youths would remember this time as a highlight of their teenage religious experiences.

The pastor invited the officers and the counselors over to his house one evening for some dessert to evaluate the work camp. They all felt the event had gone well. Most of the young people had cooperated in the schedule and very few problems had arisen. As they sat around munching on cookies and ice cream, the pastor was surprised to hear one student officer exclaim, "The work team was a great experience. But even more memorable for me will be our meetings together. It's been great fun working with all of you." This comment started a torrent of remarks by almost everyone. They all shared with each other how good the experience of working together had been. As the pastor reflected on the meeting, he said to himself, "I never would have guessed that the planning could be as meaningful as the program itself."

This illustrates a common attitude on the part of religious leaders: that the product (the service or program offered to the public) is more important than the process (the interaction members go through in planning and producing the product). The truth is that although religious organizations produce programs designed to increase faith, for the participants the process of producing those programs is of equal importance to their faith development. Religious organizations produce ministries (programs and services) through group members who work together to accomplish the tasks that turn the plans into reality. Just as workers on the assembly line at Ford Motor Company work together to produce automobiles, so members of religious groups collaborate to produce worship services, Bible study groups, social services, vacation church schools, musical concerts, and the like. The intent of all these programs is to deepen the religious experience of those who participate in them, but the paradox is that those who plan and put on the programs may find their religious experience deepened even before the event occurs. To them, the process is as important as the product. Both consumers and producers deepen their experience, not just one or the other.

Leaders who conceive their roles only in terms of the final outcome may well miss the deepening of faith that results from designing and developing the program long before the curtain goes up. While guiding the congregation, leaders should remain mindful of this truth and direct their attention to both the producers and the consumers.

Paying Attention to the Process

Sometimes the process of planning a church program is seen as part of the religious experience only in retrospect, as was the case for those who planned the work camp. However, it is also possible— and desirable—for church leaders and members to value the process as much as the product all along the way. At the very least, this means striving, in any joint effort, to treat one another in a manner reflecting religious ideals. Taking a cue from Galatians 5:22, which states that religious people should be known by their "love, joy, peace, patience, kindness, generosity, faithfulness, gentleness, and self-control," those taking part in developing a program or event can try to model these virtues in their interactions as a path to deepening their religious life.

Certainly, religious persons taking part in any process should act morally. Kant's contention that religion is essentially a matter of ethics is foundational in most people's thinking about religion. Kant's moral imperative, suggesting that we should do unto others as we would have them do unto us, is the essence of religion. It is true that, as noted in the last chapter, the process of running a religious organization doesn't always live up to religious ideals. In these cases, leaders open themselves up to charges of hypocrisy—all the more reason to pay as much attention to the process as to the product.

The California/Pacific Conference of the United Methodist church adopted some rules for dealing with the controversial subject of homosexuality that illustrate paying serious attention to the process. At their annual meeting they decided to hold several gatherings to discuss the issue. In planning what would occur during these events, the leaders recommended that everyone follow these guidelines in interacting with each other:

- We will speak with respect *to* each other, *of* each other, and *about* people [who are not here].

- We will do our best to understand and express our own feelings on the subject of sexuality.

- When we speak, we will resist the natural desire to convince others that we are right. Instead we will simply say what we ourselves have experienced, have read, or believe—and leave it at that.

- We will be brief.

- We will listen carefully to what others say.

- We will keep confidential anything that a group member has said that might embarrass him or her if it were repeated outside the context of the meeting.

These guidelines, adopted from the denomination's study material on homosexuality,[1] show that the group intends to pay as much attention to the process as to the outcome. They are moral guidelines, in the best sense of the word.

Leaders of organizations whose motive is religious, but whose work isn't, experience the product/process paradox differently from leaders of congregations. In these cases, what may be called for is to incorporate religious activities into the process. A good example of this occurs at the Bright Son Eye Hospital in Seoul, Korea. This hospital was built and is staffed by Christian ophthalmologists from Ewha University who wanted to express their faith by offering services to the poor. The nurses who work alongside them are also motivated by religious faith. For all of them, operating on diseased eyes is an act of Christian compassion. These doctors and nurses begin each morning with a devotional in a chapel that was built in the hospital for this very purpose. Although they sing songs and hear words of devotion, their prayers are for skill in doing the various tasks required in operating on eyes.

Leaders of religious businesses face yet another version of the product/process paradox. They often conceive of their daily duties as a religious call, and they expect the company's process to differ from that of the same type of business in the secular world even though the product may not differ all that much.

I heard a story about a new CEO of a church supply company. He was convinced that the process of producing religious materials should be different from that of producing secular supplies. What did he mean by this? In one sense, producing pews involves the same processes as building chairs for the home. Whether the product is the Bible or *Popular Mechanics*, publishing is the same. Writing articles, laying out copy, printing pages, and binding manuscripts has to follow in lockstep fashion before any publication comes off the press. However, the CEO was focusing on the way employees related to each other as they went about their tasks, not on the products themselves. A difference in the quality of their relationships was what he had in mind. To help the workers become aware of the religious dimension of how they worked together, the CEO thought that the least he could do would be to set up a situation where workers would worship together once a week. However, in this case his ideas about infusing the process with this kind of religious activity weren't uniformly well received by the employees.

What happened was this. The new CEO had been on the job for only ten days when he sent out a message to all employees over voice mail: "Beginning next week, we will all meet together in the dining room for devotionals every Monday morning at 8:15." In the CEO's thinking, having regular devotionals was what a good religious company should be doing. "After all," he thought, "we are a Christian enterprise. People expect us to be different. How we relate to each other in producing these goods is just as important as what we publish. At the very least, we Christians ought to pray together on a regular basis."

When Monday morning came, every employee was there. At 8:15, the CEO stood up and explained why he had initiated the Monday morning devotional time. Then he passed out sheets of paper with some scriptures and hymns written out on them. Everybody joined in; afterwards the CEO returned to his office feeling that, at last, he had made the company truly religious.

Things went well for about a month. Almost nobody missed the Monday morning devotionals. The CEO selected a new person to lead each week, mostly supervisors at one level or another in the company, since it made sense to the CEO that the leaders should set a good religious example in the company. But then attendance began to slack off. More and more workers didn't make it every week, and some no longer came at all. The CEO couldn't understand it. Since they were a company that produced religious supplies, he reasoned that everyone who worked for the company would appreciate having a devotional to begin the week. After all, they were like a family and, as the old saying goes, "The family that prays together, stays together."

He decided to ask several people to meet with him and share what they knew about the workers' reactions to the Monday morning devotionals. He was taken aback by what he heard. Almost everyone had initially applauded the devotional idea, but reported comments showed how they had become increasingly dissatisfied:

"I don't like to be told to come to worship."

"If I want to pray, I'll do it on my own time."

"I have more than enough to do. Taking time away for hymn singing puts me behind all day."

"I get tired of hearing the bosses sermonize us."

"This is not a church; it's a business."

"If they want to be religious, let them give me a raise. I need that more than religious talk."

Apparently, although some people who work in religious businesses would prefer that religious activities be part of the process, for others it's enough simply to be working on a religious program or product. The loyal group that continued to attend the Monday morning devotionals at the church supply company probably shared the CEO's thinking about process. They wanted the way they worked together to be religious in and of itself. Many of them may have chosen originally to work at Barnabas *because* it produced religious materials. They would feel called to be there. They would welcome Monday morning devotionals. They would have high expectations about the explicit religious process in their day-to-day interactions.

Others felt differently. Yes, this was a company that produced religious products, but it was primarily a business. Forget the type of product; forget the fact that the pews, the choir robes, and the books were all religious; they could just as well have been in the process of publishing *Newsweek* or manufacturing school supplies. And work was just good, hard work—it was neither religious nor nonreligious.

The CEO was caught in a dilemma. At the very least, he could have called a company meeting. He could have shared his intentions and invited reactions. This way, everyone could have been brought into the discussion and experienced both sides of the para-dox. As always, the important thing is not so much the decision that is made one way or the other, but that the paradox be admit-ted and faced. (Later I consider some other options religious lead-ers can try out in dealing with this tension.)

Valuing the Product

It may be true that many participants in religious groups care less about what the group does than about how people relate in the process. Yet a total emphasis on process can lead to failure to pro-duce anything. A congregation offering no programs would not be a church. Such a congregation might "*be* everything but *do* nothing."

As noted earlier, it's arguably common in a religious organiza-tion for the product to be valued by leaders more than the process. Even though this should be corrected by greater attention to the process, the value of the final product shouldn't be deemphasized. This is because the majority of persons in any congregation are basi-cally consumers. They are involved only tangentially in the inter-nal interactions that go into planning and putting on events. What they see about religion is what they get when they attend the pro-grams (the products of the planning). It should never be forgotten that religions exist in a marketplace and consumers are always com-paring products. Thus, as far as possible with the available resources, what religious groups do should be of high quality.

As mentioned earlier, religious leaders live with the pressure of high expectations stemming from the ideals that they, and those with whom they work, espouse. At the same time, they are running an organization that provides goods and services to the public. There may be times when the quality of what they do must be safe-guarded at the cost of the relational ideals to which they aspire. For example, sometimes it's a good idea to fire someone when he or she is underperforming, even if it seems un-Christian to do so. The problem that leaders face in situations like this is how to combine sound business concern for product quality with religious compassion and understanding.

An example had to do with a church janitor. After the death of one janitor who had been there twenty years, congregational leaders advertised the position in the town's weekly newspaper. The only applicant was a widow who lived just two blocks away but had no telephone. Some of the leaders wanted to hire her because she was a member of the church and needed the money, but others were hesitant because she had been fired from the local hospital for not being thorough enough in her cleaning and because she would be hard to contact without a phone. Besides, they questioned whether it would be a good idea to hire a member of the church. Still, they decided to offer her the job—and soon came to regret their decision. Her predecessor had been obsessively clean, but she left tasks undone, forgot on more than one occasion to open the building (and then couldn't be contacted for lack of a phone). She seemed offended when members complained. The pastor tried to work with her and shape up her performance because he knew she needed the money and she was a faithful member of the congregation. But the last straw came when it was discovered on the morning of a church fair that she hadn't cleaned up the church hall after a luncheon held three days before. Everyone had to pitch in quickly and rearrange the hall. At a meeting the next week, the leaders decided to let her go. Compassion over her situation had to give way to the need to have the janitorial work done properly.

The need to value the product is perhaps even more apparent in businesses such as the church supply company described earlier. People may assume that something produced by a religious company is not of the same quality as a product made by a secular company. Perhaps they think that religious faith is more important to the workers than savvy or skill is, but is there really any reason for thinking so? In fact, the opposite ought to be true: people should know that if a product comes from a business with a religious foundation, its quality will be as good as any other. I often ask my students, "If you're flying to New York, would you prefer to have a good pilot who is only somewhat religious or a religious person who is only a so-so pilot?" Naturally, they would prefer the former (although they would most prefer a pilot with top-notch skills *as well as* religious faith). I tell these students, who are training for religious professions, that there's no excuse for their services (that is, their product) to be anything but high quality. This is both theologically and practically as it should be.

Setting high performance standards can manifest carrying one's faith into daily work, a topic on which many sermons are preached. No matter what the occupation, one can pray to do quality work of which God would be proud. Whether the product is children or marriage, beer or boats, telephones or trucks, community or neighborhood, the producers can put high demands on themselves out of a sense that God has given them that task to do. In this way, producing a quality product can come to seem like a form of worship.

Living with the Product/Process Paradox

The product/process paradox is always present in religious organizations. In many groups the tension is rarely admitted. In these groups, which side of the equation receives emphasis differs from time to time, and somewhat haphazardly. The important thing for leaders is never to forget that the paradox is present, and to consider the possibility that people within a group may be experiencing a situation differently from one other. Even though the group members may appear to be acting in concert, and even though feelings of cohesion may be high, each person always experiences the group individually and idiosyncratically. The experience is colored by life events and whatever else is happening at the time. This is just the way things are.

When *process* is understood to refer to how people work together to accomplish tasks and reach goals, it is always true that the *product* of a religious organization is affected by those interactions. This may be denied, but nevertheless it is true. The Christian church has posed the question "Is the efficacy of the Sacrament changed by the character of the priest?" Although the Roman Catholic view has been that it is not, other groups who hold less miraculous views of the ritual have contended that it is. Further, they have added that the efficacy of almost everything that congregations do can be affected by the character of those who do the planning and the way they work with one another.

Thus, the initial act of religious leadership should be to correct any overemphasis on production—a tendency far too common in religious organizations. Leaders should announce at the first meeting of committees, "We are going to try to show our faith as much in how we work together as in what we do." The announcement may eventually find only partial realization, but it is at least a statement of intent. This same statement of intent should be communicated to the congregation at large, as well as reiterated again and again to the committee members.

Next, the intention should be monitored. Committee members and parishioners should be encouraged to let leaders know how they think such attention to process is going. Everyone should become "process conscious."

I can recall a good example of process consciousness from my adolescent years. Although I was a Methodist, I grew up in a house behind a large Baptist church, and I often attended the Baptist Training Union (BTU) that met every Sunday night. At the beginning of each meeting, someone would be appointed as critic. It was the critic's job to reflect on the process and, at the end of the meeting, to suggest ways it might be improved. A different critic was appointed each Sunday night. In this way, all who attended the meetings acquired the skill of becoming process conscious. As I think back on those meetings, what strikes me is an awareness of the importance of the process. I have often thought that it would be a good idea for every group to select a critic.

Lest these steps should be perceived as deemphasizing the final product, let me say that the importance of quality in what a religious group does should likewise be affirmed. Product must not become neglected as process has been in the past. Leaders can teach congregations the "language of product and process" and hold these in equal balance. Ideally, this will result in solid planning at the same time that process relationships are monitored. The best that can be hoped for is self-aware attention to the issue in a manner that is communicated to the members of the organization as widely as possible.

Note

1. Adapted from *The Church Studies Homosexuality*, 1994, p. 5.

9

Mission and Maintenance

Moving the Congregation Toward Achieving Its Goals While Fostering Goodwill and Group Cohesion

For years, the faculty members of the Divinity School at Yale University were too busy with their teaching tasks to attend to the deterioration of the buildings in which they taught. The university administration failed to put money into deferred maintenance as time went by. By the early 1990s, dry rot had begun to eat at the window sills, water was dripping in around the edges of the slate roofs, hardwood floors had become scarred, and paint was chipping off crumbling plaster. Suddenly everyone became alarmed. The new dean stated that his prime role would be to raise money for redecoration and restoration. When the university turned its attention to the situation, its first thought was to close the school and tear down the buildings. Only after much discussion did Yale decide to preserve part of the old campus and maintain the school.

The lesson is clear: buildings have to be maintained or they deteriorate. Perhaps not as apparent but nonetheless just as true is the fact that organizations have to be maintained or they, too, deteriorate. This maintenance has to be attended to at the same time that the "real business" of the organization is pursued. Although maintenance may seem like a sidetrack, it is essential for the healthy functioning of the organization. Both the organization's mission and its maintenance must be looked after if the organization is to thrive.

This paradox is just as true for a church organization as it is for any secular organization: time must be spent maintaining the cohesion of the group as well as pursuing the church's mission. Even though this truth is well known to religious leaders, it is disliked and resisted. Asked to spend time maintaining the organization, many religious leaders respond as Nehemiah did when he was exhorted to stop building the wall of Jerusalem: "I am doing a great work and cannot come down" (Nehemiah 6:3). As Dittes implied in the title of his book *The Church in the Way*, leaders often think that their members get in the way of achieving religious goals. One minister expressed this feeling well when he said, "I wish there were a tunnel connecting my study and the pulpit. I would traverse this tunnel every Sunday and preach my sermon. Then, without having to have contact with anyone, I would duck down into the tunnel and not be seen again until another week had passed. Church work I like; church members I hate!"

This preacher is not alone. Many leaders would like not to have to deal with people. People have opinions. They express themselves. They get into disagreements. People don't always do what they are told. When they do, sometimes they don't do it well. People cause problems. They try to please. They get angry. They get hurt. Still, this minister needed a wake-up call. He could never accomplish his dream of preaching without someone preparing the bulletin, turning on the public-address system, leading the singing, or taking up the offering.

This paradox springs from the very nature of the church as an organization. Organizations accomplish goals through people whose cohesion in working together (or lack of it) determines their success (or failure). One observer put it this way: "The church is an organization whose aim is to make known the judgment and grace of God through those whose lives are being changed by the judgment and grace of God." Religious groups are organizations, not institutions such as families that exist whether they're kept in good repair or not. Religious organizations flounder and die without maintenance and repair. The challenge is for religious leaders to realize that an investment in maintenance pays off in terms of enabling the organization to pursue its mission. It could be argued that in religion, maintenance may be the real mission.

The Mission of the Congregation

As idealistic enterprises, congregations have a mission unlike that of any other organizations in existence. Certainly, this is the conviction that guides most religious leaders. Uniqueness springs from the core fact that religion is grounded in a covenantal relationship with God and in a belief in the divine will.

Religious persons—at least those in the Jewish, Christian, and Islamic traditions—believe that they participate in a covenantal relationship with God. In return for God's blessing, they have established a profound commitment to live according to his will. Further, they strongly believe that God does, in fact, have a will, or "plan of action," regarding the way life should be lived. Most important, religious persons believe that humans have direct access to the will of God. As Plato contended many centuries ago, humans are able to purposefully envision and live in terms of an ideal world that transcends daily reality. Through prayer (the Jewish/Christian adaptation of Plato's "reminiscence"), religious persons can intuit and commit to God's will.

The fact of religion's grounding in covenant and divine will means that religious leaders act with an authority that is different from that exercised by leaders in industry, education, or government. They are not undertaking mundane tasks; they are involved in a business that transcends the ordinary—they are on a commission from God. As the ritual of one Protestant church suggests, "The Church is of God, and will be preserved to the end of time. All of every age and station stand in need of the means of grace which it alone supplies."

The mission of the congregation, grounded in the covenant and undertaken in accord with the divine will, can perhaps best be summed up with this answer given by the prophet Micah to the question "What does the Lord require of you?": "To do justice, love mercy, and walk humbly with thy God" (Micah 6:8). Little could be added to such a proclamation by leaders of any religious organization. Certainly, three of the world's great religious traditions (Judaism, Islam, and Christianity) honor these admonitions, and other religions would not find them offensive.

Justice, mercy, and humility are the primary aims of religious organizations wherever they may be found and by whatever name they may be called. One could subsume under these aims the mission or purpose of Habitat for Humanity, the Methodist Committee on Overseas Relief, the Holy Spirit Association for the Unification of World Christianity, the Hillel Foundation, the Billy Graham Crusade, the Islamic Association on the UCLA campus, Temple Yeshiva of Reform Judaism, and the Roman Catholic church. I believe that even the Rising Sun Buddhist temple would agree with Micah's statement of mission, with an ever-so-slight alteration of emphasis!

Working for equity and justice, showing mercy and compassion, and encouraging humility and spiritual growth are the basic reasons religions exist. Call them ministries; call them goals, services, purposes, or missions; call them ideologies, paths to enlightenment, or whatever you like—they are the noble motives behind all religious acts. They are the responsive intentions that flow out of the religious impulse wherever it is found.

Congregations as Organizations

All religious leaders face the reality, however, that to do justice, to love mercy, and to walk humbly with God require something more than good intentions. Accomplishing these aspirations requires an organization. As I have repeatedly stated, organizations are groups of people who come together to accomplish goals no one person could accomplish alone. Organizations are invented; they do not come into being by themselves. To belabor the point, it could be said that religious organizations are created to induce justice, mercy, and humility; they accomplish these goals through persons acting together.

Obviously, individuals can act justly, mercifully, and humbly by themselves, but the effects of their actions are very limited and the social support they need to sustain their intentions is minimal when they act alone. Most religious acts have to be planned, coordinated, and conducted by those who agree to take charge of the event and stimulate others to follow. For example, on a year-round basis, the Benedictine Monastery near Pear Blossom, California, hosts pilgrims seeking solace and spiritual growth. The monks invite retreatants to join them in celebrating as they worship several times during the day. These services, with their readings, chants, incense, candles, and such, don't just appear; they are planned and executed by people. Again, every Sunday visitors to the Full Gospel Church on Yoido Island in Seoul, Korea, find special seats equipped with earphones where they can hear any of the eight Sunday services translated into their own language. This ministry would never happen apart from behind-the-scenes planning and organization. Somebody has to assemble workers, plan strategies, assign roles, acquire materials, and monitor progress. One further example: when the press announces that the celebration of Ramadan will end with a massive celebration in Mecca, you can be sure that Muslim officials are scurrying around at that very minute planning the details of the gala event.

Even those persons who say they don't believe in organized religion join groups that are organized despite their claims of *disorganization*. The Movement for Spiritual and Inner Awareness, a Hindu-based group where each member has a confidential, individual relationship with the Spiritual Master, is a movement in which persons can grow at their own pace and in their own unique manner. Yet the group's Spiritual Master could never handle the crowds and training classes that are offered without the help of many members who do the behind-the-scenes work. Organization is a necessary component of religion, whether groups define their focus as individual or not.

This is an important realization for religious leaders as they attempt to deal with the mission/maintenance paradox. Religions are organizations, not natural institutions, and the distinction is an important one in terms of what is required of leaders. Institutions are conglomerates of persons that appear on the social scene without prior planning and whose function is agreed upon after the fact. Organizations, in contrast, are deliberately arranged, consciously conceived, structurally planned assemblies of persons brought together to accomplish goals. Organizations and institutions are often confused, and some of their processes seem similar. But organizations are intentionally planned while institutions are not.

Along with the fact that religion requires organization comes the absolute necessity of paying attention to explicit goals and plans, and of coordinating groups of people to get things done. If one relegates religion to one of society's basic institutions, like the family, these characteristics are lost. Families can exist without paying much attention to goals and strategies, but religions cannot—at least not as they are known in the Western business world. Churches are more like businesses than like families, although some leaders enjoy claiming that church members are "one big happy family."

The Need for—and Resistance to—Maintenance

In spite of their idealistic mission, and because they are organizations, religious groups are like automobiles: they require maintenance in order to run well. Although *nobody* likes to do maintenance, becoming emancipated from maintenance is always an elusive goal, both for cars and for religions. The salesperson's claim that "these diesel motors have been known to run more than 400,000 miles with few or no repairs" is appealing but should fool no one. Like organizations that always run smoothly, maintenance-free cars are forever the exception rather than the rule.

However, just like the owners of automobiles, many religious leaders don't want to spend time on maintenance. They would prefer to be driving on the open road with the wind in their face; they would prefer to be acting mercifully, fighting injustice, or preaching passionately. They would prefer to assume that people are following them enthusiastically and without any thought for their personal needs. Typically, leaders tend to become impatient when their followers do not comply quickly and fully with every request. Leaders tend not to understand when parishioners' commitment varies from time to time and day to day.

To attempt to understand maintenance in organizations, it is helpful to think of the group's members as the gears of a machine. Gears wear out, run down, lose their edge, behave erratically. Human beings stop work, put their own needs ahead of group goals, bind with others to form cliques, interfere with other people, and get stretched beyond their ability to rebound. While leaders should definitely pay attention to keeping their buildings in good repair, keeping persons harmoniously working together is far more important because even the best maintained structures are empty shells without people to bring them to life. Through the years, although the buildings were crumbling, the interaction of its distinguished faculty members with one another kept Yale Divinity School alive and well.

This inevitable need for "member maintenance" seems to pose a unique problem for religious leaders. Even if leaders of religions agree that every organization requires attention to maintenance as well as mission, they might also think this applies more to secular groups than religious ones. They might believe one or more of the following fantasies: (1) members of religions are so dedicated to the religious cause that they totally sacrifice any personal needs they might have—that is, they do not *want* the leader to spend time on maintenance; (2) religious people live in harmonious, peaceful love with each other, so they don't *need* maintenance; or (3) even where relationships break down and members get into brouhahas with one another, intentional maintenance will not be *needed* because in religion reconciliation and renewal take place automatically. All of this is to suggest that in religious organizations, leaders often think maintenance takes care of itself.

As plausible as these three fantasies might be in principle, they are still just fantasies. Even in religion, people remain people. And people are what God created them to be: self-centered containers of consciousness who have been given the task of "having dominion" in the world (Genesis 1:28). Even if persons take seriously this duty to "have dominion," they will still have personal opinions; they will perceive events differently. Even under the best circumstances they have different ideas about how to promote justice, love mercy, and walk humbly—those goals toward which all religions aspire. To top it all off, they tire, gossip, dislike, approve, befriend, and associate with one another in totally unpredictable human ways.

Even more to the point, the members of religious organizations frequently become defensive when their ideas are not adopted. The *stress* of problem solving can, and often does, become the *distress* of self-protection in conflict. When persons' self-esteem becomes so threatened that they cease working for the good of the group and become primarily concerned about themselves, leaders truly have a maintenance problem. At the very least, it takes action on the part of leaders to cohere members with different opinions into an organization composed of persons with a common purpose.

"Easter Sunrise," a case study written by Louise Weeks for training pastors, gives a good example of the need for a pastor to enter into and handle a maintenance problem. In this case study, the Rosses, a couple who are relatively new youth counselors at a church in the medium-sized community of Centerville, Florida, are given the task of planning an Easter sunrise service. In an effort to make the event inclusive, the counselors invite the local Pentecostal and black Baptist churches to join them in preparing for the service. This raises the ire of some of the old-timers in the congregation, who challenge the Rosses over the invitations. "Neither of these groups have ever been invited before," asserts Joe Black, who owns the furniture company where Mr. Ross works and who becomes so upset that he threatens to fire Ross and withdraw from the church. What should the pastor, Reverend McKinney, do? Here the case study ends, because it's meant to be a springboard for students to suggest alternatives.

Among the options that have been presented to me is one in which Reverend McKinney calls the Rosses and Black to a meeting at his house. He recounts the chronology of events that have led up to the crisis and asks the youth counselors and Mr. Black to state their concerns in turn. After each has made a statement, the pastor asks them to quiz each other and see if they can understand the concerns. Black feels that including the Pentecostals and the black Baptists will start a riot and hurt business. The Rosses feel that their friends in both groups would have been offended if they had not been invited. After the pastor is convinced that both parties understand each other, he invites them to offer suggestions of what to do next. The Rosses agree that they should have inquired into what had happened in the past and checked with church officials before extending the invitations. Black agrees that they cannot rescind the invitations and that these groups are fellow Christians who should be there. The evening ends with good feelings all around. Although in real life the situation wouldn't necessarily end there, in this resolution the pastor shows that he has some good skills of the type needed to maintain a church organization.

It is true that any kind of maintenance might look as though it takes precious time away from what leaders feel is the real purpose of their organizations. While maintenance is being performed, leaders may think that the group is inactive, that the ship is drifting, or that the car is in the garage. But almost all leaders wake up over time to the fact that they must attend to people issues. This awareness causes a shift in their thinking. Leaders of such diverse religious enterprises as the National Association of Evangelicals, the Southern Baptist Sunday School Board, the DaySpring Greeting Card Company, the Roman Catholic Diocese of Seattle, David C. Cook Publishers, Duke University Divinity School, the Simon Wiesenthal Center, and the World Council of Churches would all confirm that they began these enterprises thinking everyone would work harmoniously because they shared a common religious vision, only to find it wasn't necessarily so. They found out what is an almost universal fact: even in religious groups, maintenance is as necessary as mission if the goal of the organization is to be accomplished effectively.

Living with the Mission/Maintenance Paradox

Perhaps this inevitable contamination of the mission goals of justice, mercy, and humility with "people issues" misses the point. Perhaps the members of the organization should be the prime focus of the mission of the organization. Maybe religious organizations are unique places where members, those who supposedly produce programs to further the church's mission, are consumers as well. Could it be that the first mission of religion is maintenance of a group of persons who themselves experience justice, compassion, and humility?

These ideas are valid possibilities. Religion may be the only organization in society where the members, the workers toward justice and compassion and humility, have first been consumers. As the Christian Scriptures state, "We love because He first loved us" (1 John 4:19). This is the general principle: religious persons engage in acts of justice, love, and humility because they have experienced justice and love and they have been humbled by being blessed. Their motivation is a response to what has been done for them. They are motivated foremost by their own experience and less by compliance with leaders or by absolute identification with the task at hand. Keeping the experience of members alive and fulfilling may look like useless nurture from a distance, but it is the very lifeblood of religious organizations because their members are motivated by thankfulness rather than force or material gain. Maintaining the internal life of the organization may be, in a paradoxical sense, the best way leaders can accomplish their mission.

Like leaders in religious organizations, members feel called by God into their participation. They are going about holy business. They, too, have a sense that they have received a blessing from God and thus are willingly trying to follow God's commands by their involvement in the group. This makes their opinions, collaboration, ideas, and even disapproval take on a more profound character than what is expressed in more mundane situations.

For example, in most neighborhood churches, only a handful of the workers are paid for their time. Most are volunteers. Dittes suggests that the prime task of pastors is to present church members with opportunities to respond to God's compassion toward them. In Christian jargon, this means that the pastor's prime role is to ask every member what job he or she wants to undertake in response to God's mighty action on the person's behalf through the life, death, and resurrection of Jesus Christ. The presumption here is that every Christian is called to respond in some practical way; every member is supposed to be a minister. This implies "the priesthood of all believers," as Luther proclaimed.

If we assume that mission and maintenance are one and the same task in religious organizations, then the prime goal of leaders should be to help members find their particular ministry within the larger goals of doing justice, showing mercy, and walking humbly with God. Paradoxically, this means that the measure of whether the mission of a religious group has been accomplished should be the degree to which its members feel fulfilled in their response to God, rather than in the objective, external criteria of accomplishments. In this way mission and maintenance are united. In fact, the definition of a good organization might be "a group of persons who come together to accomplish a task that fulfills their lives."

These efforts by leaders to attend to the self-fulfillment needs of their members could be called engaging in "developmental ministry." Making ministry development the foremost role of leadership implies that the major part of the leader's time should be spent working with individual members, helping them find a task to do, and planning a lifetime career of ministries in which they will be involved. The resources of the organization should be directed toward supporting each individual in these activities. This may seem like a cart-before-the-horse approach to organizational life, but it could become normative for religious groups. In fact, although the lofty ideals of justice, mercy, and humility remain as the goals of most, if not all, religious organizations, leaders must never forget that people are the means by which such objectives are to be accomplished. The cohesion that they hope typifies their efforts toward these ends will always be an outgrowth of the sense in every individual that they are following the will of God for their lives.

The challenge of this approach lies in the inevitable reality that the religious organization must still produce programs for consumers. It cannot deal solely with the internal feelings of its members and stay in business for long. Some tasks must be completed; some programs must be produced; some events must be marketed and sold to consumers. Perhaps the best that leaders can do is be intentional about maintenance as they work toward accomplishing goals, while never forgetting that even their best intentions may not be totally accomplished.

10

Conclusion

Leading Others to Double Vision

The paradoxes we have considered in this book are implicit in all religious organizations. They come with the territory. They are part of the organizational culture. They are as real as the more formal aspects of the organization, such as its leadership chart and its explicit procedures and rules. Furthermore, they are persistent—they do not go away. My guess is that the paradoxes of religious culture that we have explored here will still be the same a hundred years from now, because that is the nature of organizational culture: it changes ever so slowly, if at all.

I have discussed eight of these persistent paradoxes. There are probably more, and I hope that this discussion stimulates readers to extend the list. My greater hope is that by consciously and intentionally facing these paradoxes, religious leaders might become more effective. As a rule, the best way to deal with organizational culture is to make explicit what is implicit. Freud said it this way: "Where Id was, there shall Ego be." Where paradoxes were part of the assumed woodwork of religious culture, they are now laid out on the table for all to see.

It is strategic to remember what I have repeatedly asserted: that these paradoxes are to be acknowledged and addressed, not resolved and laid aside. They are not problems to be solved, but rather dilemmas to be lived with. It is the "living with" that I have tried to emphasize in this volume. I believe this means moving from single vision to double vision, from an either/or to a both/and style of leadership. Accepting the truth of both sides of each paradox is where the possibility of effective leadership lies. If these paradoxes are faced and worked with, they have the potential to moderate extremes and help leaders and followers better understand one another.

Building the Religious Organization to Last

In *Built to Last: Successful Habits of Visionary Companies*, James Collins and Jerry Porras ask their readers to imagine that they meet a remarkable person who can look at the sun or stars anytime during the day or night and state the exact time and date. They note that such a person would be held in high esteem and honored by all. They ask, however, if it wouldn't be even more amazing if this person could build a clock that would do the same thing whether the person was around or not, alive or dead. Of course, the answer is yes.

Collins and Porras contend that this story has serious implications for the way business leaders should function. They should shy away from any miraculous, once-in-a lifetime feats of leadership. Instead, they should aim toward building an organization that would be self-renewing no matter who the leader was. This recommendation is based on what the authors found in their survey of companies that had achieved to a level far beyond their competitors: their success was *not* due to a charismatic leader or a great idea but was instead firmly based in the creation of companies that were, themselves, the vehicles for their success. What industrial moguls such as Charles Coffin, first president of General Electric, left to posterity was not their names or their ideas but their companies.

I am convinced that leaders of religious organizations should embrace the same aspiration. I believe that Collins and Porras's findings would be replicated were a comparison study of visionary congregations to be undertaken. Neither charismatic leaders nor novel ideas would be found to explain how those religious organizations had outperformed others. Only the organizations that had been "built to last" would stand out above the others. Creating such an organization is the most enduring contribution a leader can make.

Such a conclusion may sound puzzling since this book has emphasized the role of leadership and has implied, directly or indirectly, that success is based on the leader's awareness of the persistent paradoxes within which religious organizations must function. In proposing emphasis on the organization itself, I do not mean to deny the importance of the leader's insights. Instead, I suggest that unless these paradoxes are understood and used by the members of the organization themselves, the effect is minimal.

I believe that the greater the number of officers and members who know about and consciously work with the paradoxes, the more vital a given religious organization is. Of course, complete knowledge of these paradoxes by all members or employees is unrealistic. At the least, however, leaders should assume the role of sharing these paradoxes with as many of their officers and managers as possible. I am convinced that where this is so, the central importance of the leader diminishes and the vitality of the organization itself increases. Thus, leaders may come and go but the organization will thrive.

In teaching the management process in both church and parachurch organizations, I have used the idea of a managerial cycle to depict the skills necessary for making an idea into a reality. The following fifteen routine skills are employed over and over in sequence as a leader accomplishes tasks in any organization, religious or not:

1. Purposing
2. Discipling (making a disciple)
3. Understanding
4. Projecting
5. Involving

6. Planning

7. Committing

8. Communicating

9. Coordinating

10. Supervising

11. Marketing

12. Selling

13. Delivering

14. Evaluating

15. Recycling

In addition, leaders are occasionally required to use the skills of problem solving and conflict reduction at different points in the cycle. The cycle can be understood as passing through the phases of prescription, preparation, production, and preservation, as shown in Figure 10.1, which I use to present these concepts to my students.

Skills 2 and 3, *discipling* and *understanding,* are crucial for communication of the paradoxical features of congregational life. I think these two skills are the most important ones for building an organization that will last. In these steps, the basic conditions, visions, goals, values, and procedures of an organization are communicated to members.

Discipling refers to the time the leader spends with members introducing them to the goals, values, and purposes of the organization. During this process, members catch a vision of the way their involvement can contribute to the mission of the organization. It is here that they agree to become a part of the endeavor.

Understanding is the tempering of those purposes and plans through insight into the possibilities and limitations of organizational life. It is here that the persistent paradoxes of religious culture are shared and appreciated. It is in this phase that idealism is modulated with reality. It is here that members agree to work

Figure 10.1. The Managerial Cycle.

through the dilemmas that the paradoxes impose without becoming disillusioned. It is here that the attitude of both/and supersedes the alternative of either/or thinking—that single vision is transformed into double vision.

Members of most religious groups learn these features of organizational culture only through unintentional osmosis, because the steps of discipling and understanding are entirely neglected by the leaders. Some leaders think that putting energy into either discipling or understanding is a waste of time. To be sure, in the time that is spent explaining "how and why we do things as we do," it appears that nothing new is getting done—the organization is not producing anything tangible. But the time is not wasted, by any means. Time spent in discipling and understanding pays off in terms of both the quality and the quantity of work done later. This is a central conclusion drawn by Collins and Porras in their proposal that what visionary leaders do is build companies that last.

Following the Example of the Tournament of Roses

An organization I know well (but one not included in Collins and Porras's study) is the Tournament of Roses in Pasadena. A group composed entirely of volunteers, the Tournament does one thing and does it well: it produces the Tournament of Roses Parade and the Rose Bowl game each New Year's Day. Although the group itself is not secret, it carries on its preparations out of public view. Only on New Year's Day can the Tournament's white-suited members be seen directing traffic or riding Honda scooters darting here and there. The white suits with the group's trademark rose decals on the lapel symbolize identification with its ideals and perceptions. The remarkable feature of the Tournament is the silky smooth, unerringly traditional manner in which each annual celebration comes off in spite of the fact that the group has a new president each year and the membership continues to add new people.

The reason? Discipling and understanding, without any question. The organizational culture of Pasadena's Tournament of Roses is passed down and inculcated into the fiber of its new members before any of them moves a muscle. The Tournament spends an inordinate amount of time preparing for action by incorporating new members into its vision, purpose, and plans.

One becomes a new member by being nominated by a current member and then voted in; not every nominee is chosen. Soon after they are elected, new members are invited to Tournament House, the headquarters mansion donated to the Tournament for the first in a series of orientation meetings. As might be expected, at the first session new members are exposed to the over-one-hundred-year history of the Tournament through pictures, videos, recordings, and speeches. In the several sessions that follow, the new members are discipled into Tournament culture. They are introduced to the prime mission and goal of the annual event. Past failures as well as successes are shared and interpreted. A mentor is assigned to each new member to guide him or her during the first several years. Each new member is assigned to one of the many committees and agrees to participate faithfully in that committee for at least three years. The Tournament considers the task of discipling an integral part of building loyalty in old members as well as new ones.

Since becoming a member of the Tournament is such a coveted honor for Pasadena's citizens, there is the possibility that new members will be starry-eyed and overeager to strut the streets in white attire. The Tournament sobers their impulsiveness through understanding. Once again, a full picture of how the Tournament works is shared: its goals, successes, failures, limitations. By the time new members have cooled their heels in these extended meetings, they are ready to go about their duties with true appreciation for what can, and cannot, be accomplished through their efforts. They know well the truth that organizations are human creations that are intended to attempt tasks members could never accomplish alone. They are fully aware of the grandeur—and misery—of organizational life.

The Tournament of Roses considers each moment spent in discipling and understanding to be an essential investment that pays off grandly in behind-the-scenes planning and in staging the events on New Year's Day. They are not wrong in the least. I am convinced that this attitude is even more essential in religious organizations if those organizations want to last beyond the latest charismatic preacher or innovative program idea.

Sadly, my experience is that discipling is a much-talked-about but rarely practiced process in religious circles—except when it is applied individually rather than organizationally. Much emphasis is being placed on "spiritual development," in which congregational members are encouraged to seek out a spiritual director who disciples them individually in their private and personal religious growth. Unfortunately, little has been made of the kind of organizational discipling that can be seen in the Tournament of Roses. I continue to think this is true even though readers might point out examples of discipling efforts in their organizations. Most culturally approved religious groups implicitly depend on societal acceptance as a substitute for discipling. They assume that everyone knows who and what they are and that there is no perennial need to reincorporate persons into religious culture. But there *is* such a need—of this I remain convinced.

Nor has the value of understanding in organized religion been recognized to the extent that it is seen as a legitimate leadership skill worth developing. Unfortunately, even among religious leaders, the "organization" part of religion is very often seen as a necessary evil. However, it should be asserted repeatedly that organizations are absolutely essential for accomplishing the religious task in life. Organizations are not optional. This is why spending time on understanding is important, lest members expect too much or too little of organizational life. The persistent paradoxes in this book need to be emphasized and noted again and again, among as many members as possible, so that church life does not run itself down a dead-end street. I hope that readers will take this recommendation to heart.

References

Anonymous, "I Sought the Lord." *The United Methodist Hymnal*. Nashville, Tenn.: United Methodist Publishing House, 1989.

Beit-Hallahmi, B. "Religion as Art and Identity." *Religion*, 1986, *16*, 1–17.

The Church Studies Homosexuality. Nashville, Tenn.: The United Methodist Publishing House, 1994.

Collins, J., and Porras, J. *Built to Last: Successful Habits of Visionary Companies*. New York: HarperCollins, 1994.

De Pree, M. *Leadership Is an Art*. New York: Doubleday Bantam, 1989.

Dittes, J. *The Church in the Way*. New York: Scribner, 1967.

Endo, S. *Silence*. (W. Johnston, trans.) New York: Taplinger, 1980.

Etzioni, A. *Modern Organizations*. Upper Saddle River, N.J.: Prentice-Hall, 1964.

Handy, C. *The Age of Paradox*. New York: McGraw-Hill, 1994.

Kelley, D. *Why Conservative Churches Are Growing: A Study in the Sociology of Religion*. New York: HarperCollins, 1977.

Kennedy, J. F. *Profiles in Courage*. New York: HarperCollins, 1983. (Originally published 1956.)

Kienzle, W. X. *Chameleon*. New York: Ballantine, 1992.

Lichtman, S. L. *Ministerial Effectiveness as a Function of Personal Preferences and Job Expectancies*. Unpublished doctoral dissertation, Graduate School of Psychology, Fuller Theological Seminary, 1987.

Malony, H. N., and Hunt, R. *The Psychology of Clergy*. Harrisburg, Pa.: Morehouse, 1991.

Mouw, R. *Consulting the Faithful: What Christian Intellectuals Can Learn from Popular Religion*. Grand Rapids, Mich.: Eerdmans, 1994.

St. Augustine. *The City of God*. In *Basic Writings of St. Augustine*, vol. 2. New York: Random House, 1948.

Wallace, W. L. *Satisfaction and Stress in Ministry*. Unpublished doctoral dissertation. Nashville, Tenn.: George Peabody College for Teachers, Vanderbilt University, 1978.

"Walnut Avenue Church." Cambridge, Mass.: Intercollegiate Clearinghouse, Harvard University, 1973.

Weeks, L. "Easter Sunrise." Cambridge, Mass.: Intercollegiate Clearinghouse, Harvard University, 1975.

Index

Abingdon Press, 79
Abortion debate, 59
Acceptance by others, as ministerial motivation, 21
Accommodation approach, 27–28
Activities of religious leaders, 21–22; congregational expectations of, 24–25
Administration: approaches to, 99–101; church members' emotional reactions to, 90–92, 96–99; integration of pastoral care with, 99, 100; person/organization paradox and, 90–92, 96–101; product/process paradox and, 112–114. See also Person/organization paradox
Administrator role, 22, 34; confounding of, 35–36. See also King role
Age of Paradox, The (Handy), 12
Allport, G., 91–92
American Association of Theological Schools (AATS), 55
Amos (prophet), 48
Anglican church closures, 80
Armstrong, H. W., 47
Art, religion and, 52–53

Balance, 7
Barth, K. 2–3, 4, 7, 70–72
Beit-Hallahmi, B., 37, 38, 52
Beliefs: explicit acknowledgment of, 54–55; inclusivity/exclusivity paradox and, 52–55; timely/timeless paradox and, 59–72; truth-value and, 52–54. See also Timely/timeless paradox
Benedictine Monastery, Pear Blossom, California, 121
Berger, P., 37, 38
Bible: literal and contemporary interpretation of, 59–72; in Methodist quadrilateral approach, 65–68; reading of, sequence for, 70–71. See also Timely/timeless paradox
Billy Graham Crusade, 120
Birmingham-Southern College, 75
Boards: expectations of, 24–25; and financial decision making, 84–85; role of, in dealing with paradoxes, 131–133. See also Congregational expectations
Both/and versus either/or thinking, 6–8. See also Double-vision leadership; Living with paradox
Brennan, W., 60–61
Brigham Young University, 82–83
Bright Son Eye Hospital, 109
Brooks, P., 33
Budget dispute, 89–90

Budgeting systems, 85–86
Built to Last: Successful Habits of Visionary Companies (Collins and Porras), 6–7, 130

Callings, religious, 19–22; and leadership approach, 20–22; natural versus special, 19–20
Chameleon (Kienzle), 76–77
China, missions to, 81
Choir director firing, 96–98, 100–101
Church in the Way, The (Dittes), 4, 118
Church members: consulting with, 57, 99–100; as consumers, 126–128; emotional reactions of, 90–92; group maintenance and, 122–128; importance of process to, 105–112, 114; motivations of, 91–94; and person/organization paradox, 89–101; power of, 46–47; self-fulfillment of, 126–128; self-interest of, 91–94, 123–124; voluntary participation of, 46–47, 92–93. See also Congregational expectations; Congregations; Person/organization paradox
Church membership trends, 47–49
Church of Christ, 56–57
Church of England, 80
Church Studies Homosexuality, The, 116
Church supply company, attention to process in, 109–112
City of God, The (Saint Augustine), 77
Coercive organizations, 38–39. See also High-demand groups
Coffee hour, 94–95
Coffin, C., 130
Collins, J., 6–7, 8, 130, 133
Commercial enterprises, 78–81; attention to process in, 108–112; attention to product in, 113–114; examples of, 78–79; issues of, 79–81. See also For-profit/not-for-profit paradox
Confidentiality, 5–6
Congregational expectations: of boards, 24–25; of individual members in crisis, 25–26; for leadership activities, 23–24; for leadership style, 24–26; for religious leaders, 17–19, 23–26; for religious leaders versus other leaders, 18–19, 23, 37–38; and role confounding, 31–41; self-interest in, 91–94; serving, 23–26. See also Church members; Person/organization paradox; Person/position paradox; Role confounding
Congregational ministry, 5–6
Congregational mission. See Mission

Congregations: consulting with, 57, 99–100; "downward" identification with, 55–54; inclusivity/exclusivity paradox and, 45–58; maintaining group cohesion in, 117–128; membership trends in, 47–49; mission of, 119–120; as organizations, 120–122; power of, 46–47; relationships within, 89–101; role of, in living with paradoxes, 131–136. *See also* Church members; Inclusivity/exclusivity paradox; Mission; Religious organizations

Conservative churches: and exclusivity, 47–49, 50–51; and interpretation of Scripture, 59, 60; popularity of, 47–49

Constitution of the United States, 60–61

Consultation on Church Union (COCU), 45

Consulting, with church members, 57, 99–100

Consulting the Faithful (Mouw), 69

1 Corinthians: 11:2, 65; 11:11–12, 66; 13:12, 53

Covenant with God, 119–120, 127

Creation stories, 67

Credit theory of leadership, 27–28

David C. Cook Publishers, 126

DaySpring Greeting Card Company, 126

de Laplace, P. S., 62–63

De Pree, M., 98–99, 101

Decision making: approach to, 99; financial, 84–85; love and, 96–99; person/organization paradox and, 96–99; responsibility for, 99–100; sharing decisions of, 100–101

Delusion, 52

Denominational unity, 45; and commonalities among religious groups, 49–51; discrete, 56–57. *See also* Inclusivity/exclusivity paradox

Developmental ministry, 128

Dialogue, about decisions, 100–101

Differentiation: church members' need for, 47, 51–54; leader's "downward" identification with, 55–56; open acknowledgement of, 54–55

Disaffection, 89–91, 93–94; dealing with, 99–101; love and, 94–99

Discipling, organizational, 132, 133, 134–136

Dissension, 89–91, 93–94; dealing with, 99–101; love and, 94–99. *See also* Person/organization paradox

Dittes, J., 4, 118

Double-vision leadership, 6–8, 129–136. *See also* Living with paradox

Downward identification, 55–56

Drucker, P., 92

Duke University Divinity School, 126

"Easter Sunrise" case study, 124–125

Endo, S., 81

Ends and means. *See* Product/process paradox

Ethical behavior, 107–108

Etzioni, A., 38–39

Evangelism: as ministerial activity, 22; as ministerial motivation, 21; paradox in, 2–3, 7–8

Evangelist role, 22

Exegesis, 61–64; in Methodist quadrilateral approach, 65–68. *See also* Timely/timeless paradox

Expectations, positional. *See* Congregational expectations

Experience, in Methodist quadrilateral approach, 65, 66

Exposition, 61–64; in Methodist quadrilateral approach, 65–68. *See also* Timely/timeless paradox

Financial decision making, 84–85

Fitzgerald, F. S., 6

For-profit/not-for-profit paradox, 10–11, 75–87; living with, 83–87; need for profit and, 75–76, 77–81; need for service and, 81–83; religious leaders' motivations and, 82; tensions between profit and service and, 76–77. *See also* Commercial enterprises

Freud, S., 37, 129

Full Gospel Church, Korea, 121

Fuller, C., 79

Fuller Evangelistic Association (FEA), 80–81

Fuller Theological Seminary, 53

Fundamentalism: and exclusivity, 47–49, 50–51; popularity of, 47–49; and timely/timeless paradox, 59, 60, 67–68

Galatians: 3:28, 66; 5:22, 107

General Electric, 130

Genesis: 1:27, 67; 1:28, 40–41, 124; 2:21–22, 67

Gloria (Vivaldi), 53

God, covenant with, 119–120, 127

Gospels, 70, 71. *See also* Bible; *Individual book listings*

Group cohesion: maintenance of, 117–128; tensions of, with mission, 117–119. *See also* Mission/maintenance paradox

Group relationships, 11–12, 89–101. *See*

also Mission/maintenance paradox; Product/process paradox

Habitat for Humanity, 120
Handy, C., 12
Harvard Business School, 1, 12, 34
High religion/low religion approach, 48–49
High-demand groups: love in, 95–96; popularity of, 47–48. *See also* Coercive organizations
Hillel Foundation, 120
Holy Spirit Association for the Unification of World Christianity, 120
Homosexuality debate, 60, 108
Honesty, 69
Honeymoon theory of leadership, 27
Hunt, R., 82

Identity, inclusivity/exclusivity and, 47, 51–54
Illusion, 52
Inclusivity/exclusivity paradox, 10, 45–58; church members' need for inclusivity and, 47–49, 51–55; church membership trends and, 47–49, 55; denominational commonalities and, 49–51; denominational unity movement and, 45; exclusivity defined in, 46; inclusivity defined in, 46; living with, 54–58
Intellectual motivation, 21. *See also* Scholarship
Intentional reflection, 41
Intentionality: in dealing with inclusivity/exclusivity paradox, 55–56, 57; in dealing with paradoxes, 129–136; in dealing with timely/timeless paradox, 69
Internal Revenue Service, 79
Internet, 45
Intrinsic-extrinsic (I-E) measure, 91–92
Inventory of Religious Activities and Interests (IRAI), 21, 24, 29
Investments, social responsibility in, 79–80
Islamic Association, UCLA, 120

Job description negotiation, 26–27
1 John: 4:19, 94, 126
Jonestown massacre, 96

Kant, I., 54, 107
Kelley, D., 47, 55
Kennedy, J. F., 56
Kienzle, W. X., 76–77
King role, 33; confounding of, 35–41. *See also* Administrator role; Prophet/priest/king paradox; Role confounding
Koresh, D., 63–64

Lake Avenue Congregational Church, 86

"Launching out on faith," 86
Leadership, as ministerial motivation, 21. *See also* Religious leaders; Religious leadership
Leadership Is an Art (De Pree), 98–99
Leadership styles: congregational expectations of, 24–26; influences on, 19–22
Liberal churches, and interpretation of Scripture, 59, 60
Lichtman, S. L., 29
Lincoln, A., 62
Living with paradox: accommodation approach to, 27–28; double-vision approach to, 6–8, 129–136; of for-profit/not-for-profit, 83–87; of inclusivity/exclusivity, 54–58; of mission/maintenance, 126–128; negotiation approach to, 26–27; organization's role in, 131–136; of person/organization, 99–101; of person/position, 26–29; of product/process, 114–116; of prophet/priest/king, 39–41; of timely/timeless, 68–72
Long Beach First Presbyterian Church, 80
Lottie Moon Mission, 81
Love: and decision making, 96–99; norm of, versus reality, 94–99; and welcoming newcomers, 94–96. *See also* Person/organization paradox
Love bombing, 95–96
Luke: 18:9–14, 51; 21:2, 85
Luther, M., 23, 69
Lutheran church: in Norway, hotel enterprise of, 78; in Sweden, 76

Maintenance, of congregational cohesion: importance of, 117–119, 122–126; mission and, 119–120, 126–128; organizational nature of congregations and, 120–122; resistance to, 122–126
Malony, H. N., 82
Managerial cycle, 131–133
Mass, Roman Catholic, 53
Matthew: 21:18, 77
McCoy Memorial United Methodist Church, 75
Meese, E., 60, 61
Member maintenance, 123
Methodist Committee on Overseas Relief, 120
Methodist quadrilateral model, 65–68
Micah: 6:8, 119–120
Military Table of Order and Command, 17–18
Mission: of congregations, 119–120; group maintenance and, 117–119, 122–128; paradoxes of, 11–12, 105–116, 117–128; self-fulfillment of church members as, 126–128. *See also* Mission/maintenance paradox; Product/process paradox

Mission/maintenance paradox, 11–12, 117–128; congregational maintenance and, 122–126; congregational mission and, 119–120, 126–128; congregational organization and, 120–122; living with, 126–128; tensions of, 117–119
Mission societies, 78, 81–82
Moon, S. M., 79
Moonies, 79, 95–96
Moral guidelines, for process, 107–108
Moral imperative, 107
Motivations of church members, 91–94; intrinsic and extrinsic, 91–92; mission and, 126–127; self-interest in, 91–94, 123–124; thankfulness and, 126–127
Motivations of religious leaders, 19–21, 82; for-profit/not-for-profit paradox and, 82; listed, 21; religious calling and, 19–20
Mouw, R., 69
Movement for Spiritual and Inner Awareness, 121–122
Musician role, 22, 24
Myth, 53

Napoleon, 62–63
National Association of Evangelicals, 126
National Council of Churches, 79
Negotiation approach, 26–27
Nehemiah: 6:3, 118
Newcomers, welcoming of, 94–96
Newsweek, 60
Normative organizations, 38–39
Not-for-profit, versus nonprofit, 76, 83. See also For-profit/not-for-profit paradox

Old Fashioned Revival Hour, 80
Ordination of women, quadrilateral approach to, 65–67
Organization: of congregations, 118–119; definition of, 127; importance of, 120–122; self-renewing, 130–133; skills of, 131–136. See also Mission/maintenance paradox; Religious organizations

Paradox(es) of religious leadership, 1–13; categories of, 8; as central to religious enterprise, 4–6, 129–130; congregational role in living with, 131–136; inherent contradiction in, 2–3; of leader's role, 8–9, 17–29, 31–41; major, described, 8–12; of mission, 11–12, 105–116, 117–128; persistence of, 129; of perspective, 9–10, 45–58, 59–72; of structure, 10–11, 75–87, 89–101. See also For-profit/not-for-profit paradox; Inclusivity/exclusivity paradox; Living with paradox; Mission/maintenance paradox; Person/organization paradox; Person/position paradox; Product/process paradox;

Prophet/priest/king paradox; Timely/timeless paradox
Paradoxical mind-set, 6–8; for religious organizations, 129–136. See also Double-vision leadership
Parochial schools, 76–77, 81
Pastoral care: congregational expectations of, 25–26; integration of, with administration, 99, 100. See also Priest role
Pastoral counseling, 5–6
Pastoral counselor role, 22, 24
People's Temple, 96
Performance evaluation: and church members' power, 46–47; necessity of, 40–41; resistance to, 40; and role confounding, 35, 36–37, 40–41
Performance standards, and product/process paradox, 112–114
Person/organization paradox, 10–11, 89–101; church members' dissension and, 89–91; church members' self-interest and, 91–94; living with, 99–101; love and, 94–99. See also Church members
Person/position paradox, 9, 17–29; accommodation approach to, 27–28; congregational expectations dimension of, 17–19, 23–26; living with, 26–29; negotiation approach to, 26–27; personal leadership dimension of, 17–19, 19–22. See also Congregational expectations; Religious leaders
Personal crisis, importance of ministry in, 25–26. See also Pastoral care
Perspective, paradoxes of, 9–10, 45–58, 59–72. See also Inclusivity/exclusivity paradox; Timely/timeless paradox
Plato, 119
Porras, J., 6–7, 8, 130, 133
Preacher role, 22, 24; confounding of, 35–36. See also Prophet role
Preaching, exegesis and exposition in, 61–64
Priest role, 22, 24, 33–34; confounding of, 35–41. See also Prophet/priest/king paradox; Role confounding
Princeton University School of Theology, 83
Process: ethics in, 107–108; impact of, on product, 114–115; importance of, to participants, 105–107; in noncongregational religious organizations, 108–112, 113–114; paying attention to, 107–112, 114–115. See also Product/process paradox
Product/process paradox, 11–12, 105–116; importance of process in, 105–107; living with, 114–116; paying attention to process in, 107–112, 114–115; valuing the product in, 112–114, 115–116. See also Process

Profiles in Courage (Kennedy), 56
Profit-making transactions: necessity of, 75–76, 77–81; tensions between service and, 76–77; types of, 78–79. *See also* For-profit/not-for-profit paradox
"Program neutral" approach, 39–41, 100
Program planning: organizational maintenance and, 121–122; process in, 105–108. *See also* Process; Product/process paradox
Prophet/priest/king paradox, 9, 31–41; confounding of roles in, 31–32, 35–41; living with, 39–41; reality of separate roles in, 32–34. *See also* Role confounding
Prophet role, 33; confounding of, 35–41. *See also* Preacher role; Prophet/priest/king paradox; Role confounding
Protestant Reformation, 62
Psychology of Clergy, The (Malony and Hunt), 82

Quadrilateral model, 65–68
Quality, and product/process paradox, 112, 114, 115–116

Radio Shack, 95
Ramadan, 121
Reason, in Methodist quadrilateral approach, 65, 66
"Religion as Art and Identity," 52
Religion: art and, 52–53; ethics and, 107–108; root meaning of, 61
Religious behavior: ethics in, 107–108; love and, 94–99; and mission/maintenance paradox, 123–126, 126–128; and person/organization paradox, 91–99; in process of program planning, 105–112; self-interest and, 91–94, 123–124
Religious leaders: activities of, 21–22; activities of, congregational expectations of, 24; congregational power and, 46–47; callings of, 19–22; congregational expectations of, 17–19, 23–26, 37–38; divine authority of, 119; double vision for, 6–8, 129–136; "downward" identification of, 55–56; effectiveness of, 24; involvement of, in congregational maintenance, 123–127; motivations of, 21, 82–83; of noncongregational religious organizations, 108–112, 113–114; not-for-profit attitude of, 82–83; paradoxical roles of, 8–9, 17–29, 31–41; personal styles of, 17–19, 20–22; personal truth of, 19–22; product/process paradox and, 106–107, 108–112, 114–115; and self-renewing organization, 130–133. *See also* Living with paradox; Person/position paradox;

Prophet/priest/king paradox; Roles, religious leader
Religious leadership: double vision for, 6–8, 129–136; and paradox, 1–13; paradoxes of, 8–12. *See also* Living with paradox; Paradoxes of religious leadership; Roles, of religious leaders
Religious organizations: commonality among, 49–51; denominational unity and, 45; dimensions of, 8; for-profit/not-for-profit paradox of, 75–87; inclusivity/exclusivity paradox in, 45–58; mission of, 119–120, 126–128; mission/maintenance paradox in, 117–128; noncongregational, 108–112, 113–114; versus nonreligious organizations, 5, 46–47; organizational culture of, 129–136; organizational nature of, 118–119, 120–122; paradox as central to, 4–6, 129–130; paradoxes of mission in, 10–11, 105–116, 117–128; paradoxes of perspective in, 9–10, 45–58, 59–72; paradoxes of structure in, 10–11, 75–87, 89–101; person/organization paradox in, 89–101; product/process paradox in, 105–112; role confounding and, 38–39; self-renewing, 130–133; theological basis of, 4–6; trends in, inclusive versus exclusive, 47–49. *See also* Congregations; For-profit/not-for-profit paradox; Mission/maintenance paradox; Person/organization paradox
Rising Sun Buddhist temple, 120
Rituals: attention to process in, 114–115; belief in, 53
Role confounding, 31–41; and congregational expectations for religious versus other leaders, 37–38; inevitability of, 34–39; intentional reflection and, 41; living with, 39–41; normative character of, 38–39; and performance evaluation, 35, 36–37, 40–41; "program neutral" approach to, 39–40; of prophet, priest, and king roles, 35–41; versus reality of separate roles, 32–34; and religious versus other organizations, 38–39; versus role confusion and role conflict, 32
Roles, church. *See* Mission; Religious organizations; Structure
Roles, religious leader, 8–9; confounding of, 31–41; congregational expectations of, 17–19, 23–26, 37–38; as kings, 34, 35–36; paradoxes of, 9, 17–29, 31–41; personal leadership approaches and, 17–19, 19–22; as priests, 33–34, 35–36; prophet/priest/paradox of, 31–41; as prophets, 33, 35–36; reality of separate, 32–34. *See also* Person/position paradox; Prophet/priest/king paradox; Religious leaders

Roman Catholic Church, 120; and abortion, 59; and communion, 53, 115
Roman Catholic Diocesan Council of Detroit, 76–77
Roman Catholic Diocese of Seattle, 126
Roman Catholic Mass, 53
Rousseau, J.-J., 92

Sacramental role, 22, 24. *See also* Priest role
Saint Augustine, 77, 81
Scholar role, 22, 24
Scholarship: and inclusivity/exclusivity paradox, 50–51; as ministerial activity, 22; as ministerial motivation, 21
Science, and timely/timeless paradox, 62–63
Scripture. *See* Bible
Self-fulfillment: as church members' motivation, 126–128; as ministerial motivation, 21
Self-interest: and maintenance of congregations, 123–124, 126–127; as motivation of church members, 91–94
Self-renewing organizations, 130–133
Seminary education, and inclusivity/exclusivity paradox, 50–51
Service: as ministerial activity, 22; as ministerial motivation, 21, 82–83; need for, 81–83; tensions between profit and, 76–77. *See also* For-profit/not-for-profit paradox; Priest role
Seventh Day Adventists, 63
Silence (Endo), 81
Simon Wiesenthal Center, 126
Social contract, 92
Social reform: interdenominational collaboration on, 49–50, 56; as ministerial activity, 22; as ministerial motivation, 21
Social reformer role, 22, 24
Social responsibility, in investments, 79–80
South Africa divestiture 79–80
Southard, S., 5–6, 13
Southern Baptist church, 51, 81
Southern Baptist Sunday School Board, 126
Spiritual guide role, 22, 24
Structure, paradoxes of, 10–11, 75–87, 89–101. *See also* For-profit/not-for-profit paradox; Person/organization paradox
Successful companies, 6–7, 8; self-renewing organization and, 130–133

Teacher role, 22, 24
Technology, and timely/timeless paradox, 62–63

Temple Yeshiva of Reform Judaism, 120
Theological dimension, 4–6
Theological School Inventory (TSI), 20–21, 29
Tillich, P., 37–38, 62
Timely/timeless paradox, 10, 59–72; exegesis and, 61–64; exposition and, 61–64; living with, 68–72; method for reading the Bible and, 70–72; Methodist quadrilateral approach to, 65–68
1 Timothy: 3:1, 65
II Timothy: 1:7, 6
Tony Alamo Fashions, 79
Tournament of Roses, Pasadena, 134–136
Tradition, in Methodist quadrilateral approach, 65, 66
Trends, in church membership, 47–49
Trinity Church, Wall Street, 83
Truths, timely and timeless, 59–72. *See also* Timely/timeless paradox
Truth-value, 52–54

Understanding, organizational skill of, 132–133, 134, 136
United Methodist church, 56–57; California/Pacific Conference of, 108; quadrilateral model of, 65–68
University Baptist Church, 84–85
Utilitarian organizations, 38–39

Vivaldi, 53

Waco affair, 63–64
Walker Memorial Church, 78
Wallace, W. L., 100
"Walnut Avenue Church" case study, 1–2, 13, 34
Washington Times, 9
Weeks, L., 124–125
Wesley Memorial Church, 33–34
Why Conservative Churches Are Growing (Kelley), 47
Women, ordination of, 65–67
Woodwork problems, 93–94
Word of God, 70–71
World Council of Churches, 126
World Vision, 79
Worldwide Church of God, 47–48

Yale University Divinity School, 117, 123
Yin/Yang symbol, 7

Zero-based budgeting, 85–86